RAND NATIONAL DEFENSE RESEARCH INSTITUTE

T0288586

Mali's Next Battle

Improving Counterterrorism Capabilities

Michael Shurkin, Stephanie Pezard, S. Rebecca Zimmerman

Prepared for the Office of the Secretary of Defense

For more information on this publication, visit www.rand.org/t/RR1241

Library of Congress Cataloging-in-Publication Data is available for this publication.
ISBN: 978-0-8330-9190-1

Published by the RAND Corporation, Santa Monica, Calif.
© Copyright 2017 RAND Corporation
RAND® is a registered trademark.

Cover photo by S. Rebecca Zimmerman

Support RAND
Make a tax-deductible charitable contribution at
www.rand.org/giving/contribute

www.rand.org

Preface

This report examines Mali's counterterrorism requirements in light of the evolving political context in the country and the efforts of Mali's international partners—France, the United Nations Multidimensional Integrated Stabilization Mission in Mali (MINUSMA), and the European Union Training Mission in Mali (EUTM) and European Union Capacity Building Mission (EUCAP). Although research for this report was completed in June 2015, the findings remain relevant at the time of publication (April 2017), even though the situation on the ground has continued to evolve: Jihadist groups remain active, while northern rebel groups, despite the formal peace agreement, continue to represent a significant threat to stability in northern Mali and to the country in general. Moreover, because the terrorist threat cannot be isolated from Mali's larger security problems, treating terrorism as a discrete problem and focusing on developing specific counterterrorism capabilities are unlikely to be of much value. This report instead recommends a broad approach to building Malian capabilities, focusing on basic processes, institutions, and capabilities, while working closely with Mali's other partners both to help them and to ensure a high degree of complementarity. This research should be of interest to anyone concerned with security issues in the Sahel, counterterrorism, security force assistance, and building partner capacity.

This research was sponsored by the Office of African Affairs in the Office of the Secretary of Defense and conducted within the International Security and Defense Policy Center of the RAND National Defense Research Institute, a federally funded research and development center sponsored by the Office of the Secretary of Defense, the

Joint Staff, the Unified Combatant Commands, the Navy, the Marine Corps, the defense agencies, and the defense Intelligence Community.

For more information on the International Security and Defense Policy Center, see www.rand.org/nsrd/ndri/centers/isdp or contact the director (contact information is provided on the web page).

Contents

Figures

Summary

Mali's terrorism problem is resurgent despite the 2013 French military intervention (Operation Serval), ongoing French combat operations (Operation Barkhane), and the activities of the United Nations Multidimensional Integrated Stabilization Mission in Mali (MINUSMA). Complicating the situation is that Mali's terrorist problem is intertwined with the broader conflict afflicting northern Mali—specifically, inter- and intracommunal strife between and among northern Mali's ethnic communities. Mali's terrorist threat cannot be dealt with as a discrete problem. Unfortunately, the political strife appears unlikely to resolve despite the peace agreement signed in Algiers in June 2015—in part because of the nature of the drivers of that conflict. These include economics; inter- and intracommunal rivalries, as ethnic groups and subethnic groups jockey for position; and religion. Grievances against the Malian state are real, but they are not so important as to suggest that addressing them would end unrest. Thus, the Algiers Accords should be regarded as necessary but not sufficient to bring peace.

Mali's Terrorist Problem and Past U.S. Security Assistance Approaches

The terrorist threat in Mali is too closely connected with the larger conflicts afflicting northern Mali to isolate one from the other and focus on building a discrete counterterrorism (CT) capability. The terrorists are too rooted in Malian society and derive too much strength from Mali's many problems to be regarded as an isolated problem susceptible to a targeted military response.

Mali requires a political process and an array of initiatives that address the various root causes of conflict, including economic problems and radicalization. Mali also requires the kinds of broader skills normally associated with counterinsurgency (COIN), stability operations, or basic nation building—i.e., skills geared toward improving relations between the people and the state. Attention has to be paid to unit cohesion, morale, and ethnic integration.

This differs from what was attempted by pre-2012 U.S. security assistance programs—specifically, the Pan-Sahel Initiative and, subsequently, the Trans-Saharan Counterterrorism Partnership. These programs focused on building effective CT capabilities—as understood here to denote offensive military operations. The lessons regarding why assistance did not succeed in providing the Malian forces with effective CT capabilities include a caution against focusing on elite units; the need to match tactical military capabilities with the actual requirements associated with fighting and operating in the desert; the need to sustain training over time; and an understanding that any equipment provided to Malians must be suitably easy to learn, use, and maintain.

Malian Military Requirements

The capabilities of the Malian armed forces (Forces armées maliennes; FAMa) are poor, notwithstanding several years of security assistance led by the European Union (EU). In addition to lacking the capacity to conduct relatively complex operations, Mali's armed forces suffer from a host of weaknesses. The FAMa do a poor job with respect to basic processes, such as human resources, logistics, sustainment, and training. Human intelligence could potentially be a real asset for the FAMa; however, they appear not to leverage it to the extent that they could. One urgent requirement is the need for Mali's military to become more professional or "republican" in the sense that it upholds the law and does more to bridge the gap that exists between northern populations and the state. Part of that effort is learning how better to integrate minorities into the military—above all, foreign rebel fighters. Meanwhile, the army's sister services, such as the Gendarmerie nationale and the Garde nationale, have strengths that should be reinforced and that the army should emulate. Both the Gendarmerie and Garde tend to have greater numbers of soldiers from northern minorities and are better integrated; these services reportedly are viewed favorably by northern populations, relative to the army. Their better relations with locals both enables and results from more interaction with them. The Garde also stands out for its practice of long-endurance patrols among nomadic populations, often using soldiers who are from those populations and are familiar with them and with the surrounding terrain. This practice is not a capacity the army has but would serve it well.

Mali's interest in reviving its air wing highlights the dilemma associated with helping Mali acquire capabilities in the absence of the practices required to maintain them. Any capabilities provided to Mali should be selected not just for their consistency with Malian operational requirements but also for Mali's ability to absorb technology and maintain it.

Contributions by Mali's International Partners

France, the United Nations (UN), and the EU are making important contributions to Mali, but their efforts appear inadequate rise in insecurity. Operation Barkhane is simply too small and limited in scope relative to the vast geographic area in which it operates. MINUSMA also is struggling with limited capabilities and resources in a context defined by massive geographical distances. EUTM and EUCAP are helping, but their efforts are insufficient in light of the enormity of the task. Whatever the value of these partners' contributions, it is imperative for the United States to act in coordination with them.

Possible U.S. Contributions

Aiding the Malian Military

The United States can help the FAMa bilaterally, as well as by supporting Mali's international partners—France, the EU, and the UN. The United States should act in tandem with its international partners to ensure complementarity. Beyond that, past experience of U.S. security assistance suggests that focusing on specific units and discrete CT capabilities is unlikely to prove effective. Improving Mali's armed forces across the board is consistent with the U.S. interest in boosting Mali's CT capabilities; however, the danger is that Bamako will abuse its capabilities and exacerbate its conflict with northern populations. The solution is to improve Mali's general capabilities while making a priority of addressing the military's professional or "republican" characteristics. Respect for human rights and the rule of law and appropriately recruiting and integrating northern minorities are not trivial concerns. The United States must also promote a "first things first" approach, which would mean discouraging shortcuts, such as focusing on relatively high-end special operations forces capabilities. Greater attention should be paid to the domestic security services that are part of the FAMa—the Garde nationale, Gendarmerie nationale, and Police nationale—given their strengths relative to the army. To address the terrorist threat, Mali needs strong constabulary and police forces at least as much as it requires military ones.

As for tactical capabilities, the relative success of rebels and other irregular forces in Mali, compared with Mali's uniformed services, indicates that they practice a form of warfare well suited for northern Mali's human and physical environment. Tactical mobility—the capacity to maneuver over long distances using vehicles familiar to Malians that are easy to maintain—and communication devices that are simple to use and maintain should be priorities. The Malian military could also benefit from improvements in static defense, as well as counter–improvised explosive device (IED) capability. Long-endurance patrolling is another capability with which Mali's army needs help.

Aiding Mali's Partners

Mali's international partners are helping, but the growing insecurity in Mali suggests the need for a greater effort. France is at its limit given the other demands on the French military's resources. Current U.S. contributions to Operation Barkhane—aerial refueling; intelligence, surveillance, and reconnaissance; and lift—are critical for France's ability to conduct operations. Generally speaking, more would be better. More specifically, what would help France is anything that enhances the French military's ability to cover a large geographic area. Ground forces would help, given how thinly spread French forces are. This would be a good opportunity for Regionally Aligned Forces to get experience partnering with the French. Another asset that is in particularly short supply in the French military is rotary-wing aircraft, which limits France's tactical mobility.

The UN mission in Mali similarly presents the United States with opportunities for making contributions—directly to MINUSMA or bilaterally to troop-contributing nations. Such opportunities include helping MINUSMA in counter-IED and static defense; supporting predeployment training; working bilaterally with the Western contributors, such as the Germans, who provide much of MINUSMA's operational capacity; and providing intelligence support to MINUSMA's experimental intelligence fusion cell. Finally, EUTM and EUCAP should be regarded as an opportunity for the United States to help the Malians substantively.

Acknowledgments

We would like to thank first and foremost LTC Gabriel Chinchilla for initiating and supporting this project, as well as Amanda Dory and Commander Michael Meydenbauer for helping us bring it to a conclusion. A number of U.S. and French officials have helped us conduct interviews in Mali and in France. We would like to thank, in particular, Lt Col Douglas Brock and SFC Cameron Westphal at the U.S. Embassy in Bamako, whose help was invaluable. We also wish to express our appreciation for the support of the head of the U.S. diplomatic mission in Mali, Andrew Young. Also of great help were Colonel Bertrand Darras, Laurie Dundon, and Grégory Chauzal, who greatly facilitated our dialogue with the French government and military and made our trip to France a success. We reserve special thanks for Major General Mahamane Touré, whose support and openness to frank talk ensured our access to Mali's military leaders. A number of other people also helped make this study possible. At RAND, we are grateful to Linda Robinson and Michael Linick for their thoughtful reviews. We would also like to mention Gina Frost, Heather McLendon, Stephanie Lonsinger, Francisco Walter, and Rebecca Fowler for the editorial and administrative assistance they provided. Finally, we want to thank our friend and guide in Bamako, Ahmed Ag Abdoulaye, who reminds us of what is at stake.

CHAPTER ONE

Introduction

This study is part of a larger effort on the part of the U.S. government to assess the current terrorist threat in Mali (see Figure 1.1), delineate Mali's counterterrorism (CT) requirements, and identify ways that the United States can constructively engage with Malian security forces. The immediate background to this effort is the suspension of U.S. security assistance to Mali following a March 2012 military coup that toppled the nation's democratically elected president, Amadou Toumani Touré (commonly referred to by his initials, ATT), and the more recent decision to resume security assistance in light of Mali's return to constitutional order after the presidential and legislative elections that took place in 2013. Also in the background is the view shared by many within, and without, the U.S. government that the return on pre-2012 U.S. investments in Malian CT capabilities was disappointing in light of the coup, mass defections, and desertions among Malian security forces, as well as the serious shortcomings demonstrated by the Malian military from 2012 to the present.[1]

Our research question, therefore, is not only, "What does Mali need?" It is also "What, realistically, can the United States do to help?" and "What can the United States do differently to get a better return

---

[1] For an overview of some of the negative assessments of U.S. security assistance in Mali in light of the events of 2012, see Simon Powelson, *Enduring Engagement, Yes, Episodic Engagement, No: Lessons for SOF from Mali*, master's thesis, Monterey, Calif.: Naval Postgraduate School, 2013, pp. 3–4. Powelson notes that "commentary about the United States' security-related efforts in Mali and the region tended to categorize them as failures. "Without a doubt," he writes, the Malian army's failures and the coup "suggest anything but a successful strategy" on the part of the United States.

Figure 1.1
Map of Mali

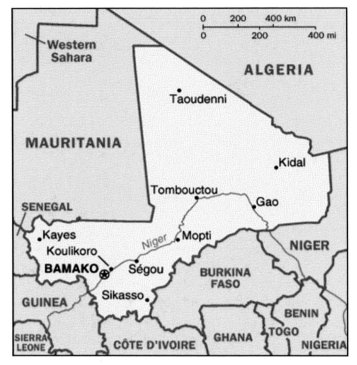

SOURCE: Central Intelligence Agency, "Mali," in *World Fact Book*,
Washington, D.C., last updated June 20, 2014.
RAND RR1241-1.1

on its investment?" To answer these questions, we divided this report
into five main chapters. Chapter Two provides background information on the conflict in northern Mali, as well as a brief overview of
the kinds of security assistance provided to Mali prior to 2012. Of
particular interest is the interconnectedness of Mali's terrorist problem and the larger set of issues associated with the country's seemingly
endless conflict with certain communities in the North. We argue that
one cannot disassociate the two problems and focus exclusively on the
terrorist threat, and past experience with providing security assistance
to Mali suggests that a narrow focus on a few specific CT capabilities

or training a few elite units is unlikely to yield much. Chapter Three examines the post–Operation Serval evolution of the terrorism and the security contexts in light of the Algiers Accords. This includes a discussion of Bamako's CT strategy. Again, we find that notwithstanding the accords, the terrorist and larger problems of northern Mali cannot be disentangled. In any event, Bamako is unlikely to focus on the terrorist threat, because it is more interested in redressing the military balance in the North. Chapter Four provides a hard look at the Malian military—its capabilities and weaknesses. Chapter Five discusses the major contributions by Mali's international partners—specifically, France, the United Nations Multidimensional Integrated Stabilization Mission in Mali (MINUSMA), and the European Union Training Mission in Mali (EUTM) and European Union Capacity Building Mission (EUCAP), which have taken the lead in training Mali's army and other uniformed security services. Any answer to the question "What, realistically, can the United States do to help?" must take into consideration what these partners are doing, their strengths, and their limitations, so as to deconflict efforts and avoid redundancies. Helping Mali might involve helping France, MINUSMA, or the European Union (EU) missions. Finally, Chapter Six pulls together recommendations on what options the United States might want to consider to build up Mali's CT capabilities.

The methods used for this study have included combining information drawn from a broad array of published English- and French-language sources, primarily U.S., French, and Malian in provenance, with insights obtained through roughly 25 semistructured interviews with individuals and groups conducted in Bamako, Gao, and Timbuktu in Mali and Creil, Lille, Paris, and Toulouse in France. In Mali, the RAND team, in coordination with the U.S. Defense Attaché's office at the embassy in Bamako, met with a selection of officers primarily in the Malian Army and Gendarmerie nationale. The team also met with U.S., French, and other European officers and civilians with direct experience working with Malian security forces, EUTM, and MINUSMA or who were directly involved with policymaking in Paris, as well as civil society members sought out specifically for their outside perspectives on the state of Mali's security sector. The research team used a number of resources relevant to security sector assessments, among them the Defense Sector Assessment Rating Tool (DSART), developed by RAND in 2010. Overall, the team relied on publicly available sources and inputs from Mali experts to guide its research.

This study was completed in June 2015. Although there have been a number of developments, both positive and negative, relating to the security situation in Mali and the evolution of Mali's military between then and the time of publication (early 2017), this analysis has retained its validity and its relevance.

A note about terminology: Mali's armed forces (Forces armées maliennes, FAMa) technically include the two services charged with external defense (the army and air force) and the three national internal security services—the Gendarmerie nationale, the Garde nationale, and the Police nationale. Colloquially, however, the term *FAMa* is used to denote the army and air force exclusively or the army alone. The inexactitude of the term often generates confusion, as many sources, including *Jane's*, fail to distinguish between the army and the other services. To avoid confusion, in this report, we use *FAMa* in its literal sense, to refer to the ensemble of Mali's five *armed forces*, and *army* when referring specifically to that service. This report, moreover, focuses on the army but discusses the other services when relevant to note important differences and particular capabilities.

CHAPTER TWO

Background to Mali's Terrorist Problem

Understanding the nature of the terrorist threat in Mali, as well as the country's difficulty in mounting an effective response, requires considering the context in which Mali's terrorists operate and, in particular, the interconnections between the country's terrorist problem and its larger security problems. It is a central thesis of this study that the terrorist problem is nested within the larger security problems and cannot be treated separately, either analytically or with respect to security policy and security sector reform: One cannot simply identify discrete CT requirements and address them through security assistance programs, at least not with any expectation of success. CT capabilities are insufficient and, in many cases, ill suited for a situation that requires broader capabilities, such as those associated with counterinsurgency (COIN), stability operations in general, and basic nation building. These capabilities are detailed in such U.S. military publications as Joint Publication 3-24, *Counterinsurgency*, and Field Manual (FM) 3-07, *Stability Operations*.[1] For example, the former argues that "the primary objective of any COIN operation is to foster development of effective governance by a legitimate government," and that "counterinsurgents achieve this objective by undertaking appropriate actions and striving for a balanced application of both military and nonmilitary means as dictated by the situation." FM 3-07 similarly argues that the objective, ultimately, of stability operations is building the legiti-

---

[1] Joint Publication 3-24, *Counterinsurgency*, Washington, D.C.: Joint Staff, November 22, 2013; FM 3-07, *Stability Operations*, Washington, D.C.: Headquarters, Department of the Army, October 2008.

macy of the government, which involves winning the confidence of the people and responding to their needs. These and other doctrinal guides make clear that actual fighting is but a small part of the kind of operations required. Past experience with security assistance in Mali further underscores the limited value of a narrowly focused training program and points to some potential best practices.

This chapter provides some background on the divisions that straddle Mali's society and how they relate to the important distinction between "north" and "south." The chapter presents a summary of the conflicts experienced by Mali since its independence in the early 1960s—up to, and including, the most recent war, which started in 2012—and how these events relate to the terrorist threat. The two last sections of this chapter examine what drives insecurity in Mali, as well as the efforts undertaken prior to 2012 by the United States to help Mali build its capabilities against terrorist groups.

A Diverse and Divided Population

As detailed in our previous publications, *Toward a Secure and Stable Mali* and *Achieving Peace in Northern Mali*,[2] Mali's division between north and south is best understood as a porous boundary between two climates (desert in the North and subtropical in the South, with the Sahelian belt in the middle) and two broad patterns of populations. In the South, where roughly 90 percent of Mali's 15.5 million inhabitants live, one finds a number of communities dominated by the Mandé, who also dominate Mali's government and military. North of the boundary, settled and seminomadic ethnic groups—most prominently the Songhays and Peuls (Fulani in English-speaking countries)—coexist with Arabs and Tuaregs.

---

[2]   Stephanie Pezard and Michael Shurkin, *Toward a Secure and Stable Mali: Approaches to Engaging Local Actors*, Santa Monica, Calif.: RAND Corporation, RR-296-OSD, 2013; Stephanie Pezard and Michael Shurkin, *Achieving Peace in Northern Mali: Past Agreements, Local Conflicts, and the Prospects for a Durable Settlement*, Santa Monica, Calif.: RAND Corporation, RR-892-OSD, 2015.

All four groups speak different languages: Songhay, Peul, Arabic, and Tamasheq (for Tuaregs).[3]

Each population group is further divided internally. For Tuaregs, at the top of the system is a (usually elected) chief, known as an *amenokal*. The dominant Tuareg confederation since the beginning of the 20th century has been the Kel Adagh. The Kel Adagh owe their dominance almost entirely to the French, who allied with them roughly a century ago against the then-dominant confederation.[4]

There are similar divisions among Mali's Arab communities, which historically have had their own confederations, complete with noble and vassal tribes, warrior elites, and religious elites. The two major Arab groupings are the Berabiche and the Kuntas (the former are predominant in the Timbuktu region, the latter in Gao). Another Arab grouping of note is the so-called Tilemsi Arabs, who inhabit the Tilemsi valley to the northwest of Gao. Mali's Songhay communities have a more horizontal organization: They are organized by villages in which elders elect village chiefs.[5] In contrast, Peul society, traditionally, has been at least as stratified as Tuareg society.

Race and Islam have historically significant roles in discourses of power in northern Mali. All northern Malians and almost all southern Malians are Muslim.[6] Arabs and Tuaregs, generally speaking, consider themselves to be "white," whereas the other communities—the Songhay, Peuls, and several others, including the Mandés—regard themselves as "black." Racial identities are based less on skin color than on

---

[3]   There are no reliable data available indicating the ethnic and racial breakdown of northern Mali's population.

[4]   Further details of the French relationship with the Kel Adagh can be found in Charles Grémont, *Tuaregs et Arabes dans les forces armées coloniales et maliennes: Une histoire en trompe-l'oeil*, Note de l'Ifri, Paris: Ifri, 2010; and Pierre Boilley, *Les Touaregs Kel Adagh: Dépendances et révoltes—du Soudan français au Mali contemporain*, Paris: Karthala, 1999.

[5]   Ronald Wesley Niezen, *Diverse Styles of Islamic Reform Among the Songhay of Eastern Mali*, dissertation, Cambridge, UK: Cambridge University, 1987, pp. 37–38.

[6]   A small minority of southerners is Christian or animist. Jews lived in northern Mali and, particularly, in Timbuktu as late as the 19th century.

ethnic and religious credentials rooted in legends describing descent from Muhammad himself or Arabs close to the Prophet.[7]

Inter- and intracommunal competition in northern Mali often leads to conflict and plays an important role in the several "northern rebellions" that Mali has experienced since its independence.

North-South Tensions

Mali's often-described "Tuareg problem" has roots in centuries-old historical antagonisms between and among various communities. Generally speaking, on the eve of Mali's independence in 1960, northern and southern Malians knew little of one another and did not regard themselves as belonging to the same country.[8] Nascent Mali was a southern construct, and Bamako soon applied a number of economic and other policies inimical to Tuaregs, in favor of communities that traditionally had been subordinate to Tuaregs. As a result, lead clans of the Kel Adagh Tuaregs initiated a rebellion in 1963. Southern Mali's repression of that rebellion was brutal, and the exactions then committed by the army would have an enduring effect on many Tuaregs' views on the Malian government and southern Malians.[9] Afterward, the South was determined to enforce Malian unity through the military, which continued to behave poorly.[10] The officers and other administrators sent to run the North—who reportedly perceived their postings as punishment or the reflection of someone's desire to distance them politically from the center of power in Bamako—tended to treat the region

---

[7]   For a full exploration of race and the role of Islam in the construction of racial identities in Mali, see Bruce S. Hall, *A History of Race in Muslim West Africa, 1600–1960*, Cambridge, UK: Cambridge University Press, 2011.

[8]   For a good overview of the north-south divide, see Grégory Chauzal and Thibault Van Damme, *The Roots of Mali's Conflict: Moving Beyond the 2012 Crisis*, CRU Report, Clingendael: Netherlands Institute of International Relations, 2015, p. 19.

[9]   For a first-person account from a southern Malian soldier's perspective, see Amidou Mariko, *Mémoires d'un crocodile: Du sujet français au citoyen malien*, Bamako: Éditions Donniya, 2001, pp. 52–66.

[10]   Chauzal and Van Damme, 2015, p. 20.

like an occupied enemy territory and committed numerous abuses, including forced marriages.[11] Matters further degraded in the 1980s as a result of severe droughts that forced many northerners into camps run by relief organizations or to seek refuge abroad. Of the latter, a significant portion went to Libya, where some enrolled in Muammar Qaddafi's Islamic Legion and served in wars in Chad and Lebanon. Exile and military service had a radicalizing effect, giving many northerners a new identity as Malian Tuaregs, which, for some, was accompanied by a desire to transcend northern Mali's traditional hierarchies. Returning Libyan Army veterans formed the core of the movement that, on June 28, 1990, attacked a military outpost in Ménaka, setting off Mali's second Tuareg rebellion. The leader was a Libyan Army combat veteran, Iyad Ag Ghali, who would become, a few years later, the leader of the Ansar Dine jihadist group. This time, a broad array of Tuareg communities—most notably nonnoble and non–Kel Adagh clans—and Arab communities joined the fight, with the Arabs forming their own rebel group.

On April 11, 1992, the Tuareg and Arab groups and the new government signed an agreement known as the National Pact, which provided a special status for the North, transfers of power to northerners, and the integration of rebels into the Malian administration and army. Bamako also accepted reducing its military presence in the North and funneling more funds for development programs toward the North.[12] In spite of the National Pact, the North remained at war, with rebel and militia groups continuing to fight each other and the Malian Army, and it took until 1996 for violence to finally recede.

Violence resumed in northern Mali in 2006 in ways that were highly reminiscent of the 1990s rebellion, with 150 Tuareg officers from the Kidal region deserting their military barracks in Kidal,

---

[11] Chauzal and Van Damme, 2015, p. 20.

[12] *Pacte national conclu entre le gouvernement de la République du Mali et les Mouvements et fronts unifiés de l'Azawad consacrant le statut particulier du Nord du Mali*, Bamako: Government of the Republic of Mali and United Movement and Fronts of Azawad, April 11, 1992.

Ménaka, and Tessalit and taking weapons and vehicles.[13] The rebellion was brief, with the Malian government signing, within three months of the beginning of the rebellion, a peace accord with the May 23 Democratic Alliance for Change (Alliance démocratique du 23 mai pour le changement) rebel group led by Iyad Ag Ghali. A minority of the combatants rejected the peace accord and took up arms again less than a year later, in May 2007.[14] This fourth rebellion in the history of Mali received little support from the northern population and was eventually crushed by the Malian Army in January 2009, with the help of Tuareg and Arab militias.

Contrary to a common perception that conflict in the region is driven by tensions between broadly defined ethnic groups (such as Tuaregs or Arabs), perhaps the most striking detail that emerges from an examination of recent conflicts is that it is rarely, if ever, the case that entire communities rebel. Uprisings are almost always the work of a few clans or tribes acting in pursuit of specific objectives, which tend to have a great deal to do with their positions relative to other clans and tribes. Within communities, elites struggle to retain their advantage, while traditionally subordinate groups attempt to raise their status. Even in the 1990 rebellion, when a broad coalition of militant groups associated with many of northern Mali's "white" communities rose up against Bamako, the conflict quickly devolved into a general melee pitting clan against clan, caste against caste, and, most devastatingly, "white" against "black." The worst violence of the 1990s by far was the result of attacks by Malian Army–sponsored Songhay militias (known as the Ganda Koy) against Arab and Tuareg civilian populations, as well as Arab and Tuareg militias' reprisal attacks against Songhay civilians. This episode and its still-vivid memory contributed to strengthening divisions in northern Mali.

The National Movement for the Liberation of Azawad (Mouvement national de libération de l'Azawad, MNLA) emerged at the end of 2011 to take up the cause of Azawad independence and launched a

---

[13] Grémont, 2010, p. 19; Baz Lecocq, *Disputed Desert: Decolonization, Competing Nationalism and Tuareg Rebellions in Northern Mali*, Leiden: Brill, 2010, p. 391.

[14] Lecocq, 2010, pp. 398–399.

new rebellion in January 2012. The precipitating cause was the arrival from Libya of a new wave of Tuaregs who had served in the Libyan military—now leaving because of the fall of Qaddafi—many bringing arms pillaged from Libyan stores. MNLA forces, aided to varying degrees by al-Qaeda in the Islamic Maghreb (AQIM) and Mali's two Islamist groups, Ansar Dine and the Movement for Oneness and Jihad in West Africa (Mouvement pour l'unicité et le jihad en Afrique de l'ouest, MUJAO), won a number of victories against the FAMa. One worth noting was the battle for Aguelhok on January 24, after which 97 Malian soldiers were executed by their captors—triggering public outrage and a desire for revenge on the part of the FAMa.[15] In March, members of Mali's "green beret" army unit overthrew the elected government of ATT, ostensibly out of frustration with the administration's conduct of the war. The coup almost certainly exacerbated the FAMa's disarray in the North, however. The MNLA and its allies completed their conquest through the spring, while relations between the MNLA and the Islamists soured. The latter turned on the MNLA and pushed it out; by the end of June, northern Mali was almost entirely in the Islamists' hands.

Mali's Terrorist Problem

Against the backdrop of northern Mali's inter- and intracommunal strife is the story of Mali's terrorist problem and its rapid evolution from being peripheral to that strife to being deeply enmeshed in it.

The terrorist threat dates back only to 2003, when the Algerian terrorist group then known as the Salafist Preaching and Combat Group (Groupe Salafiste de la prédication et le combat, GSPC) began running operations in northern Mali primarily intended to generate revenue for activities elsewhere—above all, Algeria. The GSPC in 2007

---

[15] For a chilling account of the Aguelhok battle, see Laurent Touchard, "Guerre au Mali: Retour sur le drame d'Aguelhok," *Jeune Afrique*, October 21, 2013c.

declared its allegiance to al-Qaeda and rebranded itself AQIM.[16] For most of this time and roughly until the turn of the new decade, the GSPC/AQIM could be described as a foreign element focused on a foreign conflict (Algeria) and usually operating with little more than tacit support from local populations. GSPC/AQIM generally did not target Malians or the Malian state, which was content to leave GSPC/AQIM alone. Several observers even accused ATT and other state actors of colluding with the GSPC/AQIM, allegedly to undercut Tuareg militants but also to promote various economic interests. These observers went so far as to blame Bamako for enabling GSPC/AQIM to prosper.[17] Whatever the case may have been, northern Mali's "Tuareg problem" was relevant to its terrorist problem only in that the years of strife between Bamako and some members of some communities in northern Mali contributed to generating a security vacuum that the GSPC/AQIM was able to exploit.

The situation began to change significantly in 2007–2009, when AQIM's focus broadened to include Mali itself. AQIM increasingly conducted attacks in Mali and targeted the Malian state, obliging Bamako by 2009 to shed its reserve (or complicity, depending on one's point of view) with the terrorist group and regard it, finally, as a threat.[18]

The transition was complete in 2012, when AQIM allied with Tuareg rebels and others and joined them on the battlefield against the Malian state. AQIM's status changed from profiting from Mali's conflict with its northern inhabitants to being fully a party to the

---

[16] For a good overview of AQIM and its evolution through 2013, see Chris Chivvis and Andrew Liepman, *North Africa's Menace: AQIM's Evolution and the U.S. Policy Response*, Santa Monica, Calif.: RAND Corporation, RR-415-OSD, 2013. For a focus on the GSPC period, see Baz Lecocq and Paul Schrijver, "The War on Terror in a Haze of Dust: Potholes and Pitfalls on the Saharan Front," *Journal of Contemporary African Studies*, Vol. 25, No. 1, 2007, pp. 151–154.

[17] Stephen A. Harmon, *Terror and Insurgency in the Sahara-Sahel Region: Corruption, Contraband, Jihad and the Mali War of 2012–2013*, Burlington, Vt.: Ashgate Publishing, 2014, pp. 93, 187.

[18] In June 2009, AQIM attacked, for the first time, a representative of the Malian state, when the intelligence officer Lt.-Col. Lamana Ould Bou was killed in his home in Timbuktu. See Agence France-Presse, "Suspected Al-Qaeda Members Kill Malian Army Officer," June 11, 2009.

conflict. AQIM, moreover, had been recruiting Malians throughout this period, and several had risen to leadership positions, among them Malian Arabs and Tuaregs.[19] One might also presume that more than a decade of efforts intended to foster good relations with at least some of northern Mali's inhabitants had borne some fruit.[20] In other words, what could once be described as a foreign terrorist group focused on a foreign conflict became something far more enmeshed in the social fabric of northern Mali and a party to its cleavages and conflicts.

AQIM's prominence should not diminish the importance of two developments. The first is the rise of indigenous Islamist militant groups in northern Mali that share many of AQIM's aims and ally with it. One is Ansar Dine, a Tuareg group led by Iyad Ag Ghali, who, in the previous decade, embraced Salafist Islam.[21] The second is MUJAO, a Gao-based group that appears to have been formed by Mauritanian Arabs who broke away from AQIM but successfully attracted support from a number of Malian Arab, Peul, and Songhay communities, some of which have radicalized. The rise of Ansar Dine and MUJAO underscores the point made above: By 2012, militant Islamist radicalism had taken root in Mali and was now wholly entangled with northern Mali's myriad inter- and intracommunal conflicts. The terrorists were now of the people, or at least some of the people. Their fight had become (some) Malians' fight.

Further evidence of the overlap between Mali's terrorist and larger political problems is the emergence in 2012–2013 of two new groups with ties to Ansar Dine and AQIM. The first is the Arab Movement of Azawad (Mouvement arabe de l'Azawad, MAA), formed in 2012 by Arabs from the Timbuktu region in part as a response to the retreat of Malian security forces from the region. MAA later devel-

---

[19] Andrew Lebovich, "The Local Face of Jihadism in Northern Mali," *CTC Sentinel*, Vol. 6, No. 6, 2013.

[20] Lebovich, 2013, p. 5.

[21] On the subject of Ag Ghali's transformation from rebel to jihadist, see Joshua Hammer, "When the Jihad Came to Mali," *New York Review of Books*, March 21, 2013; and Leela Jacinto, "Africa—Mali's Whisky-Drinking Rebel Turned Islamist Chief," *France 24*, June 29, 2012.

oped a pro-Bamako faction known as MAA-Platform, with the anti-Bamako and allegedly pro-AQIM faction now referred to as MAA-Coordination. Both factions are implicated in trafficking of various sorts. The second group emerged after Serval began, when a number of Tuareg notables, including the son of the Kel Adagh *amenokal*, who had joined Ansar Dine, renounced the Islamist movement immediately after French bombs began to fall and formed what eventually became the High Council for the Unity of Azawad (Haut conseil pour l'unité de l'Azawad, HCUA).

Drivers of Conflict in Northern Mali

What is often lost in any narrative of northern Mali's conflicts is a clear sense of the drivers. Several points therefore merit highlighting. First, northern Mali's conflicts have been, at most, only partially driven by grievances against the Malian state. That is not to say that those grievances lack substance, but rather that they are not always as important, relative to other drivers, as the rebel groups' public statements indicate. On the contrary, the conflicts have been driven at least as much by internal politics and reflect the ambitions of some groups, or individuals within them, to promote themselves and their interests relative to others, often at others' expense. To a large extent, one can describe Mali's conflicts since 1963 in terms of the efforts of traditionally subordinate groups to elevate themselves and traditionally dominant groups to protect their prerogatives and maintain their status. Indeed, each of northern Mali's rebel groups, from the 1963 rebellion to the MNLA and HCUA, has been dominated by members of a single ethnic or tribal subgroup who are keen on advancing their particular interests vis-à-vis other groups, at least as much as they are interested in addressing grievances against the Malian state.

Second, economics are an important factor. Northern Mali is extremely poor; its inhabitants lead a precarious existence aggravated by climate change and the collapse of the region's small tourism industry. In this context, access to aid money or any other economic resource (trafficking, for example) becomes the object of intense competition, which often lurks below ostensibly political conflicts. Fighters flow from one movement to another depending on the economic opportunities that aligning with one side or another represents at a given movement: Ansar Dine in 2012, for example, allegedly was able to lure away from the MNLA many of its fighters simply by paying them more.[22] Similarly, fights between some Arabs and the predominantly Tuareg MNLA have an ethnopolitical aspect but may also be, to a large extent, about controlling trafficking routes.

Third, the turn by some to Islamism or "reformist" Islam, which challenges local traditional orthodoxies, adds another layer to the conflict. As mentioned above, in the Sahel, it is common for some groups to legitimate their historical domination over others by means of purported religious credentials, usually claims of descent from the Prophet or those close to him. Traditionally, subaltern groups that turn to reformist forms of Islam are in effect rejecting the orthodoxies espoused by the dominant group and thereby rejecting their political authority. Radicalization is therefore simultaneously religious and political.[23]

Northern Mali offers three clear examples of this dynamic. First, the Tuareg clan at the top of the Kel Adagh and thus at the summit of northern Mali's ethnic hierarchies, the Kel Afella, has historically justified its status based on its sharifian status—that is, its religious authority tied to its alleged descent from the Prophet. Ag Ghali's and other Kel Adagh Tuaregs' turn to reformist and radical forms of Islam is at once a political and a religious bid to subvert the authority of the Kel Afella. Second, in the Gao region, the Kunta Arabs, like the Kel Afella, have justified their historical preeminence on the grounds of their sharifian status and religious credentials. Tilemsi Arabs have long been their subordinates, to the point of paying a feudal tax to the Kuntas as recently as the past decade. According to the Mali scholar Judith Scheele, the Tilemsi Arabs, because of the wealth recently acquired

---

[22] Conversation with French defense official, November 2012.

[23] See, for example, B. F. Soares, "Islam and Public Piety in Mali," in Armando Salvatore and Dale F. Eickelman, eds., *Public Islam and the Common Good*, Leiden: Brill, 2004; B. F. Soares, "The Prayer Economy in a Malian Town (L'économie de la prière dans une ville malienne)," *Cahiers d'Études Africaines*, Vol. 36, No. 144, 1996, pp. 739–753.

by their involvement in cigarette and weapon trafficking, in 2002 felt sufficiently confident to challenge Kunta domination over them, leading to electoral confrontations and violence.[24] Their embrace of radical forms of Islam and their alignment with MUJAO is simultaneously a political and a religious rejection of Kunta authority.[25] They have also allegedly been fighting the Kuntas over trafficking routes. The conflict is thus religious, political, and economic. Third, the Peuls and Songhays in the Gao region who have radicalized are similarly challenging domination by the Kuntas and their Tuareg allies. All of this makes it difficult to infer what is meant by a community's choice of aligning with a particular group, and armed clashes may result as much from two groups having conflicting political agendas as from a fight between two neighboring ethnic communities over a waypoint on a trafficking route.

Security Assistance Prior to 2012

Following Mali's independence, a number of countries have provided various forms and levels of security assistance, most notably France and the Soviet Union. Consequently, Mali's armed forces represent an awkward hybrid of French and Soviet doctrines regarding everything from tactics to force structure. Both partners and the Malians focused on conventional capabilities and building a force designed for conventional conflicts using primarily Soviet-supplied equipment. The Malian Army during the entire period from independence to at least as late as the 1990s understood its mission largely in terms of external defense; it had a force designed more or less to fight wars against Mali's neighbors, and the army's French and Soviet tutors helped it with the conventional skills required to fight those wars. As it happened, Mali

---

[24] Judith Scheele, "Tribus, états et fraude: La région frontalière algéro-malienne," *Études rurales*, Vol. 2009/2, No. 184, 2009, p. 86.

[25] Andy Morgan, "Mali's Tuareg Rebellion," *The Global Dispatches*, March 27, 2012; Chahana Takiou, "Evolution de la situation sécuritaire au Nord: Carnage à Aguel-Hoc," *Le 22 Septembre*, January 26, 2012; phone interview with Tuareg scholar, December 5, 2012.

twice went to war against Burkina Faso, in 1974–1975 and 1985, and in both times the army can be said to have acquitted itself relatively well against a peer opponent. The army also understood its mission in terms of *sovereignty*—that is, that a sovereign nation must have a military, which is understood to look a certain way. This, too, motivated Malians to build a conventional force. The United States also provided security assistance at least as early as the 1990s, more specifically after Mali's transition to democracy in 1991.[26] U.S. security assistance programs at the time focused on helping Malian and other African militaries become more proficient at peacekeeping operations.[27]

U.S. security assistance changed significantly following the terrorist attacks of September 11, 2001, when the United States folded Mali into the "global war on terror." The first major U.S. initiative affecting Mali was the Pan-Sahel Initiative (PSI), announced in 2003. PSI was a Department of State–managed program that employed U.S. European Command–based Special Forces, and it had a budget of $7.5 million over two years, with the first $6.25 million allocated during the program's first year.[28] PSI focused on developing three light infantry companies in Mali and one each in Mauritania, Chad, and Niger and instructed them in such basic skills as marksmanship, planning, communications, land navigation, and patrolling.[29] The United States and the PSI-associated units reportedly took the lead in running to ground

---

[26] Bruce Whitehouse, "How US Military Assistance Failed in Mali," *Bridges from Bamako*, April 21, 2014.

[27] Lianne Kennedy Boudali, *The Trans-Sahara Counterterrorism Partnership*, North Africa Project, West Point, N.Y.: Combating Terrorism Center, United States Military Academy, 2007, p. 4.

[28] Jim Fisher-Thompson, "U.S.-African Partnership Helps Counter Terrorists in Sahel Region," *IIP Digital*, U.S. Department of State, March 23, 2004; Kennedy Boudali, 2007, p. 4.

[29] Donna Miles, "DefenseLINK News: New Counterterrorism Initiative to Focus on Saharan Africa," American Forces Press Service, U.S. Department of Defense, January 15, 2007; Fisher-Thompson, 2004; Lesley Anne Warner, *The Trans Sahara Counter Terrorism Partnership: Building Partner Capacity to Counter Terrorism and Violent Extremism*, Washington, D.C.: Center for Complex Operations, 2014, p. 22.

Abderrazak al-Para, the GSPC commander who, in 2003, orchestrated the kidnapping in Algeria of 32 tourists, mostly Germans.[30]

After PSI came the more ambitious Trans-Saharan Counterterrorism Partnership (TSCTP), in 2005. The still-ongoing program (Mali was excluded in 2012 because of the coup) began with a budget of $100 million a year for five years and included Algeria, Morocco, Nigeria, Senegal, and Tunisia, in addition to the four Sahelian countries involved in PSI.[31] According to Government Accountability Office studies of TSCTP conducted in 2008 and 2014, the program allocated to Mali $77.6 million over the course of fiscal years 2005–2013 (by way of contrast, the program over the same time frame allocated $45 million, $58.5 million, and $74.7 million to Chad, Mauritania, and Niger, respectively).[32]

In contrast to PSI, TSCTP was designed to be interagency and reflect a broader approach to security assistance, meaning that instead of focusing exclusively on CT-associated military tactics, it included a variety of initiatives run by USAID and other U.S. government agencies intended to boost economic development and improve justice provision and security in general.[33] TSCTP objectives include several categories of engagement: military capacity building, of course, but also "law enforcement anti-terrorism capacity building," "justice sector counterterrorism capacity building," "public diplomacy and information operations," "community engagement," and "vocational training."[34] The available information does not indicate what proportion of the money spent on Mali went to military assistance, compared

---

[30] Fisher-Thompson, 2004.

[31] Miles, 2007.

[32] U.S. Government Accountability Office, *Combating Terrorism: Actions Needed to Enhance Implementation of Trans-Sahara Counterterrorism Partnership*, Washington, D.C., GAO-08-860, 2008; U.S. Government Accountability Office, *Combating Terrorism: U.S. Efforts in Northwest Africa Would Be Strengthened by Enhanced Program Management*, Washington, D.C., GAO-14-518, 2014.

[33] Miles, 2007.

[34] Warner, 2014, p. 35.

with the various nonmilitary parts of the program, although one report says it was "more than half."[35]

Most of the actual military training work was conducted by Special Forces elements subordinate to U.S. European Command (later U.S. Africa Command, AFRICOM) and Special Operations Command, Africa (SOCAFRICA), and coordinated by the Joint Special Operations Task Force–Trans Sahara (JSOTF-TS). Those elements were usually organized as Joint Combined Exchange Training (JCET) teams or Joint Planning and Assistance Teams (JPATs).[36] JCETs and JPATs made regular rotations through Mali. Mali, until 2012, also participated in TSCTP's signature annual training event, Operation Flintlock, which enabled Malian and other TSCTP participating militaries to work closely with U.S. forces and train on skills deemed relevant for a CT mission.

The best description of the training furnished to Malian forces by the JCETs and JPATs can be found in the Naval Postgraduate School thesis written by MAJ Simon Powelson, who was involved in that effort as an Operational Detachment Alpha (ODA) commander in the 10th Special Forces Group.[37]

Powelson emphasized the poor state of the Malian Army's equipping practices and the ineffectiveness of U.S. efforts to rectify them by providing the Malian Army's Combined Arms Tactical Echelons (Echelons tactiques interarmes, ETIAs), which were roughly company-sized formations of 160 men recruited from various regiments, with complete sets of personal equipment, such as uniforms.

Overall, Powelson's main conclusion is that the problem with U.S. security cooperation in Mali was the "episodic nature" of the special operations forces (SOF) training. While SOF trainers were in-country nearly continuously, each ETIA would participate in a SOF training event only twice a year, and in the meantime, personnel within the ETIAs continued to rotate. There was little chance for skills

---

[35] Walter Pincus, "Mali Insurgency Followed 10 Years of U.S. Counterterrorism Programs," *Washington Post*, January 16, 2013.

[36] Warner, 2014, p. 29.

[37] Powelson, 2013.

to accumulate; whenever an ODA would reengage with a particular ETIA, it would have to start again from scratch and teach basic soldier tasks rather than build on previous training. Powelson concludes that although the SOF training was excellent—individual Malian soldiers benefited—the program was not generating Malian units capable of rooting out AQIM.[38] An additional conclusion from Powelson's study is that cheaper and easier-to-use equipment is often of greater value in Mali than more-expensive and more-advanced equipment.[39]

Against the backdrop of the JCET and ETIA effort, Powelson describes a parallel effort conducted by JSOTF-TS using JPATs that he regards as more effective. The effort emerged in 2010 out of a desire to improve on the ETIA approach and find ways to complement it to achieve the general objective of generating units capable of attacking AQIM. It should be pointed out that at roughly the same time, France similarly began sustained training of a single Malian unit, the 62nd Motorized Infantry Regiment (62e Régiment d'infanterie motorisé, 62e RIM), presumably with similar objectives.[40] According to the available evidence, there was no real coordination between the Americans and the French, who acted in parallel rather than in concert. A U.S. SOF commander who was involved in the JSOTF-TS efforts at the time commented that he was unaware that there was a parallel French program. Although he acknowledged that coordination might have been taking place outside his purview, he said that it was unlikely.[41]

After a series of discussions between JSOTF-TS and the Malian Ministry of Defense, both sides agreed to focus on the 33rd Paratroopers Commando Regiment (33e Régiment de commandos parachutistes, RCP), the so-called red berets who would come to grief in 2012 with their failed countercoup launched against the putschist "green berets." The idea evolved until it was agreed that, within the 33e RCP, Mali would build with U.S. help a company-sized Special

---

[38] Powelson, 2013, p. 30.

[39] Powelson, 2013, p. 25.

[40] "Mali: Des instructeurs français dépêchés pour une formation anti-terroriste," *Ennahar-Online*, April 13, 2010.

[41] Telephone interview with senior U.S. SOF officer, July 16, 2015.

Forces Company (Compagnie forces spéciales, CFS) intended to be the core of a future rapid reaction battalion. The CFS would be structured roughly like a U.S. Army Ranger company, with 152 men supported by two mobility platoons with 89 men and 46 four-wheel-drive trucks. According to Powelson, the CFS would therefore have significantly more vehicles than a standard Malian unit, reflecting a desire to endow it with greater mobility and the capability of penetrating far into the desert for extended periods of time: A unit capable of dealing with AQIM would have to be capable of doing classic maneuver warfare over large distances—that is, classic desert warfare.[42] Ironically, this was something that, as a French desert warfare manual notes, indigenous Sahelian forces, such as AQIM and Tuareg rebels, are proficient in, while Malian and other countries' government services, with their traditional proclivity toward attempting more-conventional operations with conventionally organized forces, are inept at them.[43]

Powelson describes how the JPAT's efforts with the CFS developed a three-tiered approach, with some training provided separately to lower-rank enlisted soldiers, noncommissioned officers (NCOs), and officers, with the purpose of developing their particular skills with respect to their ranks and responsibilities. NCOs, for example, were cultivated as trainers. Indications of progress were already evident in 2011. Officers and NCOs, according to Powelson, began exhibiting the kinds of leadership skills and capabilities "recognizable to U.S. Army NCOs." Moreover, at Flintlock 2011, the Malian contingent, which in 2010 had scored "at the bottom of the regional pack," were now "top performers."[44] According to Powelson, the CFS's overall record in the 2012 war was respectable. In contrast, the ETIAs almost immediately disintegrated, and their equipment passed to the enemy. The French-trained 62e RIM was also still operational but had adopted a defensive,

---

[42] Powelson, 2013, pp. 34–36.

[43] Centre de doctrine et d'emploi des forces, *Doctrine d'emploi des Forces Terrestres en zones désertique et semi-désertique (édition provisoire)*, Paris: Armée de Terre, 2013.

[44] Powelson, 2013, pp. 40–41.

static posture; it would play an important role in the initial stage of Serval, when it worked with the French to defend Konna.[45]

This overview of U.S. assistance prior to 2012 yields several insights. One is the need to provide sustained training to stable Malian units to generate forces capable of acquitting themselves competently in battle. One has to start from the beginning and then slowly and methodically work one's way toward more-advanced capabilities. Another insight is the need to address the FAMa's overall managerial and logistical capabilities and not focus on just one or a few maneuver units: If the FAMa cannot sustain a maneuver unit in the field, that unit will fail regardless of its qualities. A third insight is the value of simple equipment that is easy to learn to operate and maintain, as opposed to complex equipment that is hard to use and difficult to maintain. Advanced and expensive capabilities are likely to be wasted on Mali's security forces. In addition, there is the need to tailor training and equipping to requirements based on a realistic assessment of the country's security needs. Mali might not need armor, for example, but it does need the ability to conduct long-range maneuvers in the desert and mount coordinated attacks.

The SOF commander cited above added a note of skepticism regarding Powelson's thesis about the "episodic" nature of SOF training being at the root of the ETIAs' failures. According to the officer, both the ETIAs and the 33e RCP's CFS suffered from the same basic problem: a lack of mobility, which undermined the value of these units, no matter how well trained.[46] Without the ability to place units where they need to be and move them as required, he argues, they can accomplish little. The officer concluded that cultivating elites was intrinsically a poor investment: The entire force needs to be improved and equipped with adequate means of mobility, means that locals know how to maintain.

Lastly, it should be noted that the training provided by U.S. SOF focused entirely on tactics and planning, with little, if any, attention

---

[45] Powelson, 2013, pp. 53–54. On the 62e's role in the battle for Konna, see Laurent Touchard, "Mali: Retour sur la bataille décisive de Konna," *Jeune Afrique*, January 30, 2014a.

[46] Telephone interview with senior U.S. SOF officer, July 16, 2015.

paid to aspects of military operations that are increasingly recognized as essential in asymmetrical conflicts and stabilization operations. These include efforts to shape public perceptions, cultivate public trust, and provide any of a wide range of humanitarian services or other activities intended to generate good will and strengthen ties between the military and civilians, or even simply to cultivate an appropriately professional or republican institutional culture within the FAMa (meaning a culture that embraces promoting the values of the Malian republic and encourages improving relations with northern minorities). The FAMa prior to 2012 and after was and is a remarkably diverse force with respect to ethnicity; however, little effort appears to have been made to foster ethnic integration and unit cohesion.

The example of the Tuareg soldiers in the ETIAs who deserted or defected to the rebels in 2012 is well-known; less appreciated is the fact that Mali's military leaders and U.S. trainers alike paid astonishingly little attention to encouraging the Tuareg recruits to identify with one another regardless of their clan, ethnic, or tribal solidarities, as well as with the FAMa.[47] According to the SOF commander interviewed for this study, SOF paid little attention to developing unit cohesion or esprit de corps; their focus was on tactics. The then-commander of AFRICOM, GEN Carter Ham, corroborated, to some extent, this view in January 2013. He told a Washington, D.C., audience that U.S. forces involved in training Malian troops (who were among those who deserted in massive numbers) failed to train them in "values, ethics and a military ethos."[48] According to Ham, the United States focused "almost exclusively on tactical or technical matters," and not enough was done to convince Malian recruits that "when you put on the uniform of your nation, you accept the responsibility to defend and protect that nation, to abide by the legitimate civilian authority that has been

---

[47] Interview with senior FAMa special forces battalion officer, Bamako, Mali, January 22, 2015.

[48] "Mali Crisis: US Admits Mistakes in Training Local Troops," *BBC News*, January 25, 2013.

established, to conduct yourselves according to the rule of law."[49] At the very least, there was a need to attend to unit morale: As the SOF commander put it, the ETIAs were sent north to fight an enemy that was at least as well trained and equipped but that had a vastly greater sense of purpose. The commander suggested that U.S. SOF may not be best suited for attending to such matters as morale and unit cohesion, because SOF tend to default to a focus on tactical skills. U.S. regular Army forces, he argued, would be a better match for this task, with the Regionally Aligned Forces (RAF) being the obvious choice.[50]

Conclusion

The above overview should make clear that the interconnectedness of Mali's terrorist threat and the larger conflicts afflicting northern Mali made it impossible to isolate the one from the other and focus on building a discrete CT capability. The terrorists are too rooted in Malian society and derive too much strength from northern Mali's many problems to be regarded as a distinct problem susceptible to a targeted military response. This suggests that Mali requires a political process and an array of initiatives that address the various root causes of conflict, including economic problems and radicalization. Mali also requires the kinds of broader skills normally associated with COIN, stability operations, or basic nation building—that is, skills geared toward improving relations between the people and the state. Attention has to be paid to unit cohesion, morale, and ethnic integration. Even if one were to focus on specific capabilities, as was the case with pre-2012 U.S. security assistance, developing capabilities in a vacuum guarantees that results will be limited at best: The 33e RCP and the French-trained 62e RIM were good, but they were not enough, and the FAMa could neither keep them in the fight nor organize an effective resistance around them. This approach of focusing on elite units, more-

---

[49] Tyrone C. Marshall Jr., "AFRICOM Commander Addresses Concerns, Potential Solutions in Mali," U.S. Africa Command, January 24, 2013.

[50] Telephone interview with senior U.S. SOF officer, July 16, 2015.

over, meant that there would never be enough quality units to effect a desired outcome, and none had the kind of mobility that could compensate for small numbers. This argues for an approach more based on building the entire force than on focusing on a few select units. With respect to tactical military capabilities, care must be taken to match them to the actual requirements associated with fighting and operating in the desert. Training has to be sustained over time, so that units can learn together and that trainers do not have to start over from scratch with each training cycle. Finally, any equipment provided to Malians must be suitably easy to learn, use, and maintain, with cheap and simple often providing more value than expensive and advanced.

CHAPTER THREE

Mali Post-Serval

The French intervention of 2013 has offered Mali an important opportunity to pursue a political process while rebuilding its security forces. Indeed, Bamako's political efforts came to fruition in recent months, when the last of northern Mali's nonjihadist armed groups finally signed the new Algiers Accords, and Bamako has been pursuing a number of military reform initiatives while working closely with the new European training mission to improve the overall capability of its army.

We find, however, that the situation, in general, has improved less than what one might have hoped for in the heady first months of Serval. The terrorist threat is persistent and in some ways more ominous, given its greater geographic range and further evidence of collusion with local populations. The peace process, notwithstanding the signing of the Algiers Accords, remains fragile and unlikely to provide what Mali's international partners expected of it: to address the conflict between Mali and northern communities at least well enough to enable Bamako to focus on the CT problem (ideally with the constructive participation of local armed groups) and free Mali's international partners to focus their assistance on CT capabilities. Even if one could separate the two sets of problems, Bamako will likely persist in regarding the nonterrorist armed groups, the so-called Compliant Armed Groups (CAGs), as a greater threat to Mali than the terrorists. Lastly, with respect to the specific capabilities Bamako seeks, it appears that although some Malian military leaders are aware that they need broad, nontactical capabilities adapted to stability operations and COIN, there is still a focus on CT tactics.

This chapter examines the state of the terrorist problem since Serval and the evolution of the conflict between Mali and the various militant groups. It also looks at the development of Bamako's own CT strategy, its perspective on distinguishing between terrorist groups and the CAGs, and the kinds of capabilities it is pursuing.

Terrorism Resurgent

The terrorist threat in Mali—though remaining well below 2012 levels—has resurged. Islamist fighters who had either gone to ground or returned from neighboring countries are active again. Gone are the large, overt formations of "technicals" and heavy weapons that were a feature of the conflict in 2012. However, guerrilla-style attacks, improvised explosive devices (IEDs), and other forms of irregular warfare are becoming common in northern Mali, as well as, increasingly, the central regions of Ségou and Mopti. According to MINUSMA, levels of violence appeared to have risen in the last months of 2014 and the first months of 2015.[1] However, it is unclear, at this point, what might be causing this increase. Jihadist groups might have more recruits or more funds, or are simply quickly learning how to overcome the FAMa's, MINUSMA's, and France's defenses. Higher levels of violence during that period are also because of an increased number of clashes between armed elements from the two main groups negotiating for a peace agreement in Algiers, who are eager to come to the table in a position of force.[2]

Serval significantly diminished the Islamists' capabilities, as well as the number of their fighters. The French military sources available to us estimate the number of fighters on the eve of Serval at about

---

[1]   United Nations Security Council, *Report of the Secretary-General on the Situation in Mali*, New York, S/2015/219, March 27, 2015, para. 24; MINUSMA, "MINUSMA Deeply Concerned at Upsurge of Violence in the North of Mali," press release, May 19, 2015b.

[2]   United Nations Security Council, 2015, para. 2.

1,200;[3] the French and their allies killed roughly 200, with the remainder fleeing or going to ground inside Mali. The French have continued to conduct combat operations against the jihadists as part of Operation Barkhane, which replaced Serval in July 2014, and they are currently conducting what has been described as a decapitation strategy targeting jihadist leaders.[4] MUJAO lost of one its leaders and founding members, Ahmed al Tilemsi, who was killed in December 2014 by the French forces.[5] In March, the French killed another of the group's commanders (and former AQIM member), Oumar Ould Hamaha.[6]

Yet the Islamist groups remain active and appear to be regaining strength, slowly. As of early 2015, AQIM was estimated to have about 300 combatants, almost as many as on the eve of Serval.[7] The group has claimed responsibility for a number of attacks in the past two years, including the particularly lethal one against a Malian Army base in Nampala in January 2015.[8] AQIM is also active outside Mali. In June 2014, the group claimed responsibility for an attack against the residence of Tunisia's interior minister, which killed four policemen, as well as the June 2013 explosion in the Jebel Chaambi (a mountainous area bordering Algeria), which killed two Tunisian soldiers and wounded two more.[9] Ansar Dine, too, remains active and claimed responsibility

---

3   11th Parachute Brigade, briefing, Fort Bragg, N.C., June 23, 2013.

4   Rémi Carayol, "Terrorisme au Sahel: La stratégie de Sisyphe," *Jeune Afrique*, March 24, 2015.

5   "French Forces in Mali Kill Islamist on U.S. Wanted List," Reuters, December 11, 2014; "Mali: Un chef djihadiste d'Al-Mourabitoun tué dans une opération française," *Le Monde*, December 11, 2014.

6   Both men were on the U.S. list of wanted terrorists. "Al-Qaeda in the Islamic Maghreb," *Jane's World Insurgency and Terrorism*, October 22, 2014; "Mali: Mort d'un important jihadiste," Radio France Internationale, March 14, 2014.

7   Baba Ahmed, "Mali: Deux ans après Serval, AQMI reprend ses quartiers au Nord de Tombouctou," *Jeune Afrique*, January 9, 2015.

8   "AQIM Attack Against Malian Army Close to Mauritanian Border Indicates Group's Strategy to Stretch French Security Operation," *IHS Jane's Intelligence Weekly*, January 6, 2015.

9   Jamel Arfaoui, "Tunisia: AQIM Claim Tunisia Attack," *Magharebia*, June 16, 2014; Benjamin Roger, "Tunisie: Deux militaires tués dans une explosion au Jebel Chaambi,"

for attacks against MINUSMA camps in Kidal (September 2014) and Tessalit (December 2014).[10]

Two more groups have emerged, Mokhtar Belmokhtar's al-Mourabitoune, which used to be part of AQIM, and the Macina Liberation Front, which conducted a series of attacks in central Mali in the first months of 2015.

Al-Mourabitoune's short but bloody history goes back to July 2013, when MUJAO announced that it had merged with Mokhtar Belmokhtar's al-Mulathameen ("masked men") Brigade (also known as el-Mouaguiine Biddam—"those who sign in blood"), an offshoot of AQIM that had made headlines in 2013 by attacking (with MUJAO's help) the In Amenas gas plant in Algeria and two uranium-mining sites in northern Niger.[11] Al-Qaeda's leader, Ayman al-Zawahiri, allegedly requested the merger of the two groups.[12] The statement announcing their merger described their ambitions as extending "from the Nile to the Atlantic,"[13] which is a departure from MUJAO's West Africa–focused ambitions. Al-Mourabitoune claimed responsibility for the March 2015 attack in Bamako against a restaurant and bar popular among expatriates. The group allegedly carried out the attack in revenge for the killing, by the French Army, of Ahmed el-Tilemsi and for the cartoons of Muhammad published in the French satirical magazine

---

Jeune Afrique, June 6, 2013.

[10] "Al-Qaeda-Linked Group Claims Mali Restaurant Attack," *Aljazeera*, March 9, 2015; International Crisis Group, CrisisWatch Database: Mali, Brussels, undated.

[11] "Belmokhtar's Militants 'Merge' with Mali's MUJAO," *BBC News*, August 22, 2013. There is some confusion regarding the two names of Mokhtar Belmokhtar's group. Masked Men Brigade seems to have been the name of the cell he was leading within AQIM, before cutting ties with the group ("Those Who Sign with Blood," GlobalSecurity.org, 2015). The In Amenas attack was claimed by Those Who Sign in Blood; the twin suicide bombings of Niger were claimed by both MUJAO and Those Who Sign in Blood ("Le groupe de Mokhtar Belmokhtar revendique le double attentat au Niger," *France 24*, December 20, 2013).

[12] "Mali: Un chef djihadiste d'Al-Mourabitoun tué dans une opération française," 2014.

[13] Statement published by Mauritanian news agency ANI, cited in "Belmokhtar's Militants 'Merge' with Mali's MUJAO," 2013.

Charlie Hebdo.[14] In that same statement, al-Mourabitoune also claimed responsibility for the destruction of 25 UN vehicles and the deaths of three peacekeepers.[15] MUJAO still claims some attacks in its name only, suggesting that the group retains some measure of independence. In this perspective, al-Mourabitoune may be best understood as a forum for occasional cooperation and operational coordination rather than a new group that has replaced the two others.

The Macina Liberation Front—an apparent reference to the Peul Empire (Macina Empire) that, under the banner of Islam, conquered much of present-day Mali in the 19th century, including the Mopti and Ségou regions—started operating in January 2015 in central Mali, extending into the Gao region. This group reportedly attracts mainly Peuls, including members of MUJAO,[16] and it might be allied to either MUJAO or Ansar Dine.[17] The group is active in central Mali, where it has been going through villages to recruit young men. The group is allegedly responsible for the killing of a forest warden in Diafarabé (Mopti region), the planting of a mine that killed two Malian soldiers in Diabaly (Ségou region), and the killing of several civilians.[18] It might also be responsible for the attacks against Malian soldiers in Tenenkou

---

[14] Agence France-Presse (AFP), "Suspect in Bamako Restaurant Bombing Killed, Mali Says," *France 24*, March 13, 2015b; Sebastien Rieussec, "Saharan Islamist Group Claims Responsibility for Mali Attack," *France 24*, May 14, 2015.

[15] Rieussec, 2015. See also "Foreigners Targeted in Mali Restaurant Attack," *Aljazeera*, March 8, 2015.

[16] Interview with U.S. expert on West Africa, Washington, D.C., May 2015 (name withheld on request). We conducted many confidential interviews in the course of this assessment; we cite only the interviewee's role or title in those instances.

[17] "Mali: Lawlessness, Abuses Imperil Population," Human Rights Watch, April 14, 2015.

[18] "Mali: Qui est derrière les attaques dans le centre du pays?" Radio France Internationale, April 12, 2015; Diakarida Yossi, "Suite aux différentes incursions du Front de libération du Macina: Mopti, la Venise malienne, en état de psychose le week-end dernier," *L'Indépendant* (Bamako), April 21, 2015; "Mali: Lawlessness, Abuses Imperil Population," 2015.

in January 2015.[19] The leader of this new group appears to be Hamadou Koufa, a preacher and former associate of Ag Ghali.[20]

The persistence of these groups in the face of ongoing French combat operations and their ability to conduct operations and, apparently, recruit locals indicate that the collective threat they pose is unlikely to end anytime soon and may even grow, unless the French or the rest of the international community significantly increases CT operations in Mali. Moreover, the terrorist threat is already evolving in some dangerous ways.

A Wider Range of Targets

Prior to the takeover of the North by jihadist groups, security concerns in that area were mostly limited to two types of incidents: (1) kidnappings of foreigners by criminal groups or AQIM and (2) intercommunity clashes, often in relation to economic interests (e.g., pastoral areas, access to water and other resources, trafficking routes). These types of incidents have not disappeared: Kidnappings of foreigners in the North have been limited by the fact that few foreigners now travel to, or live in, these regions, but there have been exceptions: Two French journalists were killed in Kidal in November 2013, and, in April 2015, a Romanian national was kidnapped from a mining site in Burkina Faso, close to the border with northern Mali.[21] Intracommunity tensions have continued. In February 2014, Peul tribesmen attacked Tuareg and pro-Bamako General El Hadj Ag Gamou's home village of Tamkoutat, in what the analyst Andrew McGregor presents as "the latest stage of an ethnic conflict between local Tuareg and Fulani [Peul] herders."[22]

---

[19] Benjamin Roger, "Mali: Au moins deux soldats maliens tués dans l'attaque contre Ténenkou, près de Mopti," *Jeune Afrique*, January 16, 2015; "Mali: Qui est derrière les attaques dans le centre du pays?" 2015.

[20] "Mali: Qui est derrière les attaques dans le centre du pays?" 2015.

[21] Mathieu Bonkoungou, "Gunmen Kidnap Romanian from Burkina Faso Mine Near Mali Border," Reuters, April 4, 2015.

[22] Andrew McGregor, "A Divided Military Fuels Mali's Political Crisis," *Terrorism Monitor*, Vol. 12, No. 12, June 13, 2014.

New security concerns have piled up on these existing issues. Targets of attacks now include Malian security forces, French troops, MINUSMA peacekeepers, humanitarian organizations, and the civilian population writ large. Attacks have increased in number, and they involve a larger range of weapon types, including mines and IEDs. While insecurity used to be concentrated in northern Mali—roughly, north of the Niger Bend—it is now prevalent in central Mali (Ségou and Mopti regions) as well, with at least one deadly incursion in Bamako.

Attacks Against MINUSMA and French Troops

International forces in Mali have become a prime target of attacks by jihadists (see Figure 3.1). As of March 2015, MINUSMA counted 35 peacekeepers killed—including nine in a single attack on October 3, 2014—and 138 wounded over a total of 78 attacks.[23] MINUSMA's

Figure 3.1
Types of Targets and Numbers of Attacks Attributed to Jihadist Groups

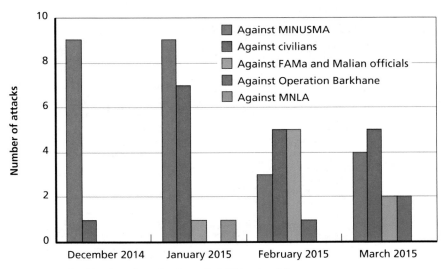

SOURCE: United Nations Security Council, 2015, para. 24.
NOTE: Figures cover the period from December 17, 2014, to March 16, 2015.
RAND RR1241-3.1

---

[23] MINUSMA, "Since the Launch of the #UN Mission in #Mali, Peacekeepers Have Been Victims of Various Types of Attacks," posted to Twitter by UN_MINUSMA, April 13, 2015a.

patrols were attacked by heavily armed gunmen or hit by IEDs and mines.[24] MINUSMA bases have also suffered mortar and rocket attacks, such as the ones that killed a Senegalese peacekeeper in October 2014 and the one that killed a Chadian peacekeeper and two Malian children on March 8, 2015, both in Kidal.[25] MINUSMA has also sustained suicide attacks, such as the April 15, 2015, one against a base in Ansongo (Gao region), which killed three civilians and wounded 16, including nine Nigerian peacekeepers.[26] MINUSMA contractors are being targeted as well. Their vehicles are looted and burned, and their personnel sometimes killed.[27] Responsibility for these attacks has been claimed by MUJAO, AQIM, and al-Mourabitoune.[28]

From January 2013 to December 2014, France lost a total of 12 soldiers in Mali, with roughly half these casualties taking place after the end of what might be called the major combat operations phase of Serval.[29] So far, MINUSMA bears the brunt of the casualties suffered by international forces in Mali, because of its greater size (8,543 peacekeepers in Mali compared with roughly 1,000 to 1,400 French soldiers),[30] as well as the fact that MINUSMA contingents are more vulnerable than the French.[31]

---

[24] See, for instance, "Mali Crisis: Attack on UN Convoy Kills Two," *BBC News*, April 18, 2015.

[25] "Mali: Une nouvelle attaque meurtrière visant un camp de la Minusma à Kidal," Radio France Internationale, October 8, 2014; "Mali: Trois morts dans une attaque contre la Minusma à Kidal," Radio France Internationale, March 8, 2015.

[26] AFP, "Nord du Mali: Attentat suicide contre une base de l'ONU, 3 morts," *Le Nouvel Observateur*, April 15, 2015d.

[27] "Another Attack on a Convoy of MINUSMA Contractors," United Nations Multidimensional Integrated Stabilization Mission in Mali, April 20, 2015.

[28] "Mali: Lawlessness, Abuses Imperil Population," 2015.

[29] "In memoriam," French Ministry of Defense, December 10, 2014.

[30] This number was as of December 31, 2014, for MINUSMA (United Nations Security Council, Resolution 2164, 2014a, Annex) and as of October 2014 for French troops in Mali (Valérie Samson, "Un dixième soldat français tué au Mali," *Le Figaro*, October 30, 2014).

[31] Rémi Carayol, "Mali: Les Casques bleus, cibles privilégiées des jihadistes," *Jeune Afrique*, October 23, 2014.

Attacks Against Malian Security Forces

Malian security forces represent another target of choice for armed groups and suffer the same types of attacks as international troops: Gunmen attack their convoys, deploy mines and IEDs against vehicles, and fire mortars and rockets at bases. A particularly deadly attack— claimed by AQIM—took place in Nampala on January 5, 2015, near the border with Mauritania, when 11 soldiers were killed and nine wounded after attackers entered their base.[32] Some attacks have also taken a more personal turn. Relatives of General El Hadj Ag Gamou (also the founder of the pro-government militia known as Imghad Tuareg and Allies Self-Defense Group [Groupe autodéfense touareg Imghad et alliés, GATIA]) were specifically targeted by an attack in November 2013, which killed two, including a three-year-old girl; Ag Gamou attributed the attack to MUJAO.[33] Unidentified assailants in January 2015 attempted to assassinate General Mohamed Ould Meydou, a loyalist Arab militia leader.[34]

Attacks Against Humanitarian Organizations

Human Rights Watch recorded attacks—which were usually motivated by financial gain—committed by either armed groups or bandits, between November 2014 and April 2015, against 13 vehicles of humanitarian aid organizations.[35] Yet, on March 30, 2015, MUJAO carried out what seems to be a more political attack against a convoy of the International Committee of the Red Cross (ICRC)—which was clearly marked as such—on the road from Gao to Niamey, killing one of the organization's employees and wounding another. MUJAO's spokesperson, Abou Walid Sahraoui, claimed that his group had killed

---

[32] "Mali: L'armée attaquée près de la frontière mauritanienne, cinq morts, " *Jeune Afrique,* January 5, 2015; "Mali: Au moins huit soldats tués, que s'est-il passé à Nampala?" *Jeune Afrique,* January 6, 2015; AFP, "Mali: Nouvelle attaque d'une localité dans le centre, un civil tué," *No. 1,* January 7, 2015a.

[33] "Mali: Au moins deux membres de la famille du général ag Gamou tués," Radio France International, November 21, 2013.

[34] David Lewis, "Top Malian Army Officer Survives Assassination Attempt in Capital: Sources," Reuters, January 26, 2015.

[35] "Mali: Lawlessness, Abuses Imperil Population," 2015.

an ICRC employee "who was working for the enemy."[36] This suggests that even the ICRC, an organization that goes to great lengths to be perceived by actors of conflict as neutral and impartial—a policy that has allowed it to access some hard-to-reach populations in need—is not treated in Mali as neutral and can be specifically targeted.[37] Whether motivated by graft or ideology, these attacks have resulted in increased risk and difficulty for humanitarian organizations to provide much-needed services and supplies in areas that are bereft of public services.

Attacks Against the Civilian Population

Malian civilians have suffered both as direct and indirect victims. Militants have targeted civilians in an attempt to gain their support or prevent them, through intimidation, from working with international and Malian forces. Militants killed more than ten people in 2014 for allegedly providing information.[38] On March 19, 2015, AQIM shot and beheaded a man suspected of spying for the French in Tichift, a village located 75 miles north of Timbuktu. The killing took place during daytime in the middle of the marketplace, clearly as a warning for the rest of the population.[39] Another armed group, the Macina Liberation Movement, was reported by Human Rights Watch to be "threatening local populations with death if they collaborated with French forces, the government, or the UN peacekeeping mission." This movement is responsible for killing at least five individuals for such motives.[40] Others have been collateral victims, killed or injured by stray bullets or mines presumably intended for MINUSMA or Malian forces. Just in

---

[36] AFP, "Après la mort d'un de ses employés, le CICR suspend ses déplacements dans le nord du Mali," aBamako.com, April 1, 2015c.

[37] The number of ICRC staff killed in attacks has ranged from one to 14 per year between 2003 and 2013, according to Humanitarian Outcomes, with the highest toll taking place in 2013 (Abby Stoddard, Adele Harmer, and Kathleen Ryou, *Aid Worker Security Report 2014: Unsafe Passage; Road Attacks and Their Impact on Humanitarian Operations*, London: Humanitarian Outcomes, U.S. Agency for International Development, August 2014).

[38] MINUSMA figure cited by "Mali: Lawlessness, Abuses Imperil Population," 2015.

[39] "Mali: En plein marché, Aqmi décapite un homme accusé de travailler pour les Français," *Jeune Afrique*, March 23, 2015.

[40] "Mali: Lawlessness, Abuses Imperil Population," 2015.

the first two weeks of April 2015, in the Gao region, two civilians were seriously injured when their vehicle hit a mine or IED, and a rocket attack killed one woman and injured three people.[41]

The general insecurity and absence of government security forces in the North expose the civilian population to a wide range of additional security threats, including assault, robbery, armed attacks on roads, extortion at gunpoint, and theft of animals.[42] Banditry is not a new phenomenon in Mali, but Human Rights Watch reports that, according to community leaders, banditry has "become particularly acute since mid-2014, after state security forces stopped patrolling." Civilians in Conflict (CIVIC) has similarly noted an increase in banditry as the result of a "security vacuum" in areas where pro-government forces and the anti-government CAGs are fighting for control.[43] Lack of a police presence (or complacency, when it is present)[44] has also led the population, in a few instances, to take the matter into its own hands. In Gao in March 2015, for instance, two men suspected of building bombs were killed by a mob.[45]

Finally, civilians are also still threatened, to some extent, by the Malian security forces themselves. Human Rights Watch reports mistreatment of detainees in custody by virtually every Malian official and unofficial security force, including the army, national guard, gendarmerie, and GATIA. The situation for detainees in custody, although still dire, seems to have somewhat improved in 2015, when compared with the two previous years.[46] CIVIC reports rates of sexual violence

[41] United Nations Office of the High Commissioner for Human Rights, "Press Briefing Note on Yemen and Mali," April 14, 2015.

[42] "Mali: Lawlessness, Abuses Imperil Population," 2015. Human Rights Watch notes that extortion at gunpoint is sometimes done by government forces.

[43] CIVIC, *Fending for Ourselves: The Civilian Impact of Mali's Three-Year Conflict*, Washington, D.C., 2015, p. 29.

[44] Human Rights Watch reports that civilians interviewed complained of poor investigation by security forces of banditry incidents ("Mali: Lawlessness, Abuses Imperil Population," 2015).

[45] "Mali: Trois morts dans une attaque contre la Minusma à Kidal," 2015.

[46] "Mali: Lawlessness, Abuses Imperil Population," 2015.

that remain high (albeit lesser than during the war) and finds that civilians who live close to military camps are particularly vulnerable to such abuses.[47]

A Wider Range of Weapons and Methods

The quantity of weapons in circulation in Mali, as well as the types of weapons being circulated, has changed with the war. Mali always had a large number of weapons as remnants of previous rebellions. During the 1990–1996 rebellion, however, weapons usually came in very small quantities from Libya or Mauritania. Most weapons used by the rebels were taken from Malian troops during attacks.[48] The recent war has changed this situation both quantitatively—a considerable number of weapons were looted in Libyan arsenals and disseminated throughout the regions—and qualitatively: An inventory of some of the arms and ammunition found in northern Mali during the war shows that there are now more types of light weapons and heavy equipment in circulation than there were following the 1990–1996 rebellion.[49] Some of these types, such as 106-mm recoilless rifles and NR-160 rockets, can be traced back to Libya.[50] Operation Serval uncovered approximately 200 tons of arms and munitions, as well as about 20 tons of ammonium nitrate to be used in IEDs, and destroyed a number of arms caches.[51] It is, however, impossible to assess how much of the overall arsenal of the various armed groups this represents, or how much these groups have been able to resupply—possibly again from Libya.

---

[47] CIVIC, 2015, p. 29.

[48] Nicolas Florquin and Stephanie Pezard, "Insurgency, Disarmament and Insecurity in Northern Mali, 1990–2004," in Nicolas Florquin and Eric Berman, eds., *Armed and Aimless: Armed Groups, Guns, and Human Security in the ECOWAS Region*, Geneva: Small Arms Survey, 2005, p. 53.

[49] This is based on a comparison between the lists of weapons in circulation established by Florquin and Pezard, 2005, p. 52; and Conflict Armament Research and Small Arms Survey, *Rebel Forces in Northern Mali: Documented Weapons, Ammunition and Related Material, April 2012–March 2013*, London and Geneva, April 2013.

[50] Conflict Armament Research and Small Arms Survey, 2013.

[51] French Ministry of Defense, *Opération Barkhane*, Paris, August 11, 2014.

Another source of concern is the increasing use of IEDs and mines, which the United Nations Office of the High Commissioner for Human Rights judges to be "very worrying."[52] As of January 2015, IEDs and mines represented the single largest source of casualties for MINUSMA troops in Mali.[53] They are also a relative novelty for Mali. Mines were not used in the 1990s and appeared in Mali only in 2007–2009, when another Tuareg rebel group—Ibrahim Bahanga's Niger-Mali-Tuareg Alliance (Alliance-Touareg-Niger-Mali [ATNM])—started using anti-personnel and anti-vehicle mines against the Malian Army.[54] But the ATNM was a small group with limited external support;[55] it is therefore unlikely that it would have managed to amass large quantities of mines at the time. The mines and IEDs (or explosives to be used in IEDs) that are now prevalent in Mali are therefore likely to have come into the country in recent years. Victims of mines and IEDs have included MINUSMA soldiers, Malian soldiers, and civilians. These devices make communication even more perilous in a country that was already beset by poor road infrastructures and connections, further jeopardizing the country's economic recovery.[56] These weapons impede MINUSMA's operations, including air operations, as some IEDs are planted near airstrips. In July 2014, a MINUSMA vehicle hit an IED at the Kidal airfield.[57]

[52] United Nations Office of the High Commissioner for Human Rights, 2015.

[53] Jeremy Binnie, "Analysis: UN Peacekeepers Struggle Against IEDs in Mali," *IHS Jane's Defence Weekly*, January 6, 2015.

[54] "Mali: Indignation Dominates Reaction as Attacks in the North Escalate," Integrated Regional Information Network, August 31, 2007.

[55] Angel Rabasa, John Gordon IV, Peter Chalk, Audra K. Grant, K. Scott McMahon, Stephanie Pezard, Caroline Reilly, David Ucko, and S. Rebecca Zimmerman, *From Insurgency to Stability*, Vol. 2: *Insights from Selected Case Studies*, Santa Monica, Calif.: RAND Corporation, MG-1111/2-OSD, 2011, p. 136.

[56] Human Rights Watch reports, for instance, the case of a transport company owner saying that one of his trucks hit a landmine ("Mali: Lawlessness, Abuses Imperil Population," 2015).

[57] Binnie, 2015.

Finally, attacks by jihadist groups have become more sophisticated over time.[58] On January 17, 2015, for instance, the joint MINUSMA-Barkhane camp in Kidal was hit by two vehicle-borne IEDs at the same time a rocket and mortar attack was going on.[59] Jihadists do not rely any more on a single mode of action, which has been contributing to the lethality of the attacks.

A Wider Geographical Reach
Armed groups in Mali have also broadened their geographic scope (see Figure 3.2). Although they no longer control any portion of Mali's territory, they remain active in a large part of the country—a larger part than the one they used to operate in before Operation Serval. Bamako was hit for the first time in March 2015, when a gunman opened fire in a restaurant, killing five people. Al-Mourabitoune claimed responsibility for the attack.[60] The accidental explosion that killed two individuals who were handling explosives in April 2015 on the outskirts of Bamako suggests that there might be more attacks in preparation.[61]

Jihadist groups still operate relatively freely in a number of well-known locations of northern Mali, such as the Adrar des Ifoghas and the area around Ménaka.[62] They have also reinvested in some of the areas from which the French forces expelled them in 2013–2114: In December 2014, AQIM fighters were spotted in large numbers in the Timbuktu area, close to the border with Mauritania.[63] Armed groups are also in areas where they did not use to be present, such as the Ouagadou forest, between Mali and Mauritania,[64] from where

---

[58] Heather Sonner and Kyle Dietrich, *Fending for Ourselves: The Civilian Impact of Mali's Three-Year Conflict*, Washington, D.C.: Center for Civilians in Conflict, 2015, p. 26.

[59] United Nations Security Council, 2015, para. 25.

[60] AFP, 2015b.

[61] Associated Press, "Explosive Detonates in Mali's Capital, Killing 2," *New York Times*, April 3, 2015.

[62] Carayol, 2015.

[63] Ahmed, 2015.

[64] Carayol, 2015.

Figure 3.2
Map of Mali with Locations of Recent Attacks, October 2014–March 2015

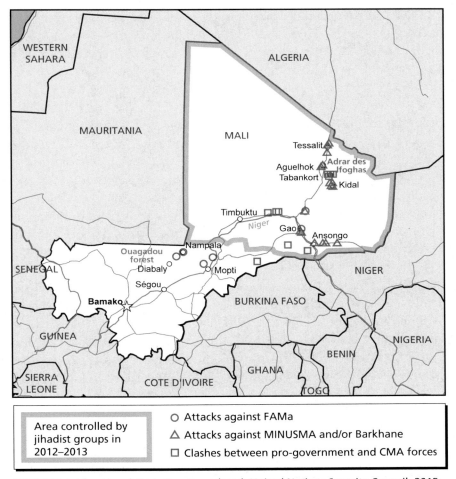

SOURCES: International Crisis Group, undated; United Nations Security Council, 2015; Massiré Diop, "Mali: Suite à de violents accrochages dimanche dernier à Boulkessi: Des éléments du HCUA chassés de la localité par l'armée malienne," *L'Indépendant* (Bamako), November 4, 2015; "Mali: Neuf casques bleus tués," *Le Monde* with Reuters, October 3, 2014.
NOTE: CMA = Coordination des mouvements de l'Azawad (Coordination of Azawad Movements).
RAND RR1241-3.2

they are likely to have launched the Nampala attack of January 2015. Although it was not the first time that Nampala was attacked—the ATNM had carried out a particularly deadly attack there against a Malian garrison in December 2008—it does bring the threat closer to Bamako (300 miles).[65] AQIM sources cited by the Mauritanian news agency al-Akhbar claimed responsibility for this operation and stated that they chose that location because of its proximity to Diabali, where Operation Serval started in January 2013.[66] Diabali is considered in the South,[67] as are the Ségou and Mopti areas that recently experienced a spate of attacks from the Macina Liberation Movement.

Jihadist groups have also established rear bases outside Mali. The region of Fezzan in southwestern Libya, in particular, is a safe haven where jihadists plan attacks, such as the one that took place in Bamako. It is from that area that Mokhtar Belmokhtar planned and launched its attacks against Algerian and Nigerien sites in 2013.[68] Libya, which is still awash with weapons from the fall of Qaddafi and the looting of the Libyan state's arsenals, is a convenient training ground for Malian jihadist groups.[69] In December 2014, French Minister of Defense Jean-Yves Le Drian called Libya a "terrorist hub," adding that Mokhtar Belmokhtar and Iyad Ag Ghali were there.[70] Abdelmalek Droukdel (of AQIM) was also reportedly seen in the country.[71] Recognizing that situation, the G5 Sahel—Chad, Mali, Niger, Mauritania, and Burkina

---

[65] As a matter of fact, the December 2008 attack had been the trigger to the decisive reaction from the Malian government, whose January 2009 offensive brought the end of the ATNM. See Rabasa et al., 2011, pp. 144–147.

[66] "Mali: Au moins huit soldats tués, que s'est-il passé à Nampala?" 2015.

[67] "Mali: Au moins huit soldats tués, que s'est-il passé à Nampala?" 2015.

[68] Carayol, 2015.

[69] Carayol, 2015.

[70] François Clémenceau, "Le Drian: 'Daech essaie de prendre la main en Libye,'" *Le Journal du Dimanche*, updated December 30, 2014.

[71] Carayol, 2015.

Faso—called that same month for an international intervention in Libya to "neutralize armed groups" operating from Libya.[72]

Another source of concern is the possibility of a linkup between Mali's jihadist groups and Boko Haram. In 2012, a UN report had highlighted that a number of Nigerian and Chadian Boko Haram militants had received training in AQIM camps during the summer of 2011.[73] In early 2013, reports emerged of a training camp in the Timbuktu area that would have hosted approximately 200 Boko Haram combatants, in addition to Malian jihadists, before the French troops took over the area.[74] Boko Haram has started increasing its recruitment in Cameroon and Niger, and the presence of international troops may be the only reason Mali is not part of the list yet.[75]

This wider geographic reach of jihadist groups suggests that Mali's CT measures should be coordinated with those implemented by its neighbors—both at the operational and policy planning levels. The importance of regional collaboration has been underlined by Sahelian countries in a number of venues—including at the ministerial meeting of African-troop contributors to MINUSMA that took place in Niger in November 2014—and by the UN.[76] The Nouakchott Process—the Africa Union–led process launched in March 2013 with the aim of increasing intelligence and security cooperation between 13 states in the Sahel and Sahara regions—was based on the idea that all these countries are subject to similar threats.[77] It remains to be seen how this

---

[72] Quoted in "Cinq pays du Sahel appellent l'ONU à intervenir militairement en Libye," *Le Monde*, December 19, 2014.

[73] Cited in Anne Kappès-Grangé, "L'ONU confirme les liens étroits entre Boko Haram et Aqmi," *Jeune Afrique*, January 29, 2012.

[74] Drew Hinshaw, "Timbuktu Training Site Shows Terrorists' Reach," *Wall Street Journal*, February 1, 2013.

[75] Emmanuel de Solère Stintzy, "Terrorisme: Quand Boko Haram recrute au Cameroun," *Jeune Afrique*, September 9, 2014.

[76] United Nations Security Council, *Report of the Secretary-General on the Situation in Mali*, New York, S/2014/943, December 23, 2014b, para. 18.

[77] United Nations, *Nouakchott Process*, United Nations Multilingual Terminology Database (UNTERM), undated. The Nouakchott Process calls for frequent meetings of its members

process will combine with existing structures, such as the Regional Command for Joint Counterterrorism Operations (Comité d'état-major opérationnel conjoint, CEMOC), created in 2010 to increase cooperation among the joint staffs of Mali, Algeria, Niger, and Mauritania since 2010. In this perspective, U.S. security cooperation in Mali should be examined in relation to other U.S. and international assistance efforts in Algeria, Mauritania, Niger, and Burkina Faso, at a minimum.

Evidence of Popular Support

The increased geographical range of terrorist incidents also underscores the fact that terrorist groups in Mali benefit from the support and collusion of some members of some communities, whose motivations include religious conviction but who are rooted in myriad economic and political issues. Terrorists operating in the Gao region, for example, often implicate radicalized Malian Peuls and Songhays;[78] the former are associated with the new Macina Front, the presence of AQIM in the Ouagadou Forest, and the attack on Nampala.[79] According to a Gendarmerie nationale intelligence officer, the Peuls of Ségou (central Mali) have ties to Ansar Dine.[80] Indeed, there are signs of ties between the terrorist groups and various relatively radical Islamic communities and preachers in central and southern Mali, including Bamako.[81] Information regarding how much support terrorist groups get from locals or the proportion of locals in terrorist groups relative to foreigners is not available; however, Mali's terrorist groups clearly are, for all intents and purposes, Malian, and one can presume that support for radical Islamist politics among Malians may continue to grow.

---

to discuss security issues (every two months for the heads of intelligence and security services and every three months for ministers of foreign affairs).

[78] Interview with Gendarmerie nationale officer, Gao, Mali, January 21, 2015.

[79] Interview with Gendarmerie nationale intelligence officer, Bamako, Mali, January 21, 2015.

[80] Interview with Gendarmerie nationale intelligence officer, Bamako, Mali, January 21, 2015.

[81] Interview with U.S. officers in MINUSMA, Bamako, Mali, January 25, 2015.

The Algiers Accords

The negotiations that finally resulted in the recent signing, in June 2015, by all parties (save the jihadist groups; see Figure 3.3) of a peace agreement represents, on the surface, the fulfillment of a desire nurtured by Mali's international partners to separate Mali's internal political problems from its terrorism problem. The hope has been to demilitarize the political contest with northern armed groups—ideally even enlisting their support for CT operations—and facilitating the return of Malian security forces to their northern posts and their conduct of CT operations.

Regrettably, such an outcome is unlikely. First, in the words of a May 2015 International Crisis Group report, "the Malian hardline, still influential in Bamako, particularly in the security and military

Figure 3.3
The Parties to the Peace Negotiations: Pro-Government Militias (Platform) and Anti-Bamako CAGs (Coordination)

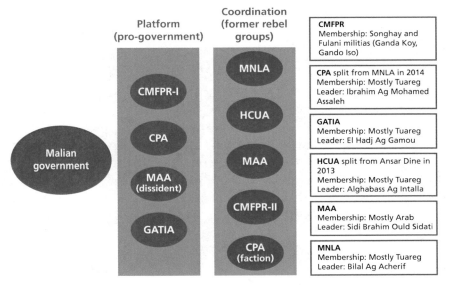

NOTES: CMFPR = Coordination des mouvements et fronts patriotiques de résistance (Coordination of Movements and Fronts of Patriotic Resistance); CPA = Coalition du peuple de l'Azawad (Azawad People Coalition). CMFPR was split into two groups.
RAND RR1241-3.3

milieu, remains animated by the desire to avenge itself against the politico-military groups in the north."[82] Moreover, these same people regard the rebel groups "not as political movements but rather as mafia groups that maintain troubling ties with the terrorists."[83] Virtually all of the Malian officers interviewed for this study emphasized that they do not distinguish between the CAGs and the terrorist groups because of overlapping personnel and a record of cooperation. As one Malian military source put it, the MNLA and AQIM might not be the same thing, but because he sees the MNLA as complicit with AQIM, there is, to him, no meaningful difference.[84] According to a senior FAMa intelligence officer,

> For the Malian security forces, it's really hard to distinguish between who is a terrorist and who is [a CAG member]. Very difficult. The two groups operate in the same space with the same methods, and they must be in communication. Ultimately, for us there's no real difference. The [CAGs] do acts that are terroristic, so we consider them terrorists.[85]

The fact that these same groups in question signed the accords in June is unlikely to change Bamako's estimation of them. Second, the purpose of the peace agreement was to address relations between north and south, meaning that other drivers of conflict remain—specifically, intra- and intercommunal political and economic competition, much of it focused around base commercial interests.

Until the CAGs demobilize and disarm, it will remain true that (1) the CAGs, militarily, have the upper hand relative to Mali's security services; (2) Bamako, because of its military limitations, relies on militias (see below) to exert military pressure; and (3) the return of a full Malian military presence in the North—called for by the accords—

---

[82] International Crisis Group, *Mali: La paix à marche forcée?* Rapport Afrique 226, Brussels, 2015, p. 9.

[83] International Crisis Group, 2015, p. 9.

[84] Interview with senior Gendarmerie nationale anti-terrorism officer, Bamako, Mali, January 23, 2015.

[85] Interview with senior FAMa intelligence officer, Bamako, Mali, January 19, 2015.

and the commencement of military operations ostensibly targeting terrorists almost certainly will keep tensions at a near boil. The bottom
line is that the current peace agreement is a necessary condition to
improving security in the North, but it is not a sufficient one.

Post-Serval Malian CT Strategy

It is fair to say that ATT's strategy for dealing with the North prior
to 2012 amounted to managing problems rather than solving them,
all the while benefiting from CT-related aid from the United States
and other nations. A case in point is the Program for Peace, Security, and Development in Northern Mali (Programme pour la paix, la
sécurité et le développement au Nord-Mali, PSPDN), a development
initiative paid for by international donors and launched by ATT in
2011.[86] Many have criticized PSPDN for being too little, too late, too
inattentive to the region's fundamental economic and social programs,
and largely a gesture intended to placate the international community.
They suggest that had ATT been serious about the North, he would
have done more, sooner, and without having to be told.[87] One can say
the same thing regarding AQIM: ATT neglected the problem until
roughly 2008–2009, when he, appealing to international help, charted
a course toward cultivating Malian military capabilities that, in retro-
spect, clearly was insufficient.

Although it is unclear whether Bamako really had AQIM in mind
as it worked with the United States and France in 2009–2011, it is
doubtful that Malian leaders, as they go about trying to build military
capabilities, are currently focused on the terrorist groups. In addition,
as of mid-2015, Mali does not appear to have developed what one can
consider a formal strategy for dealing with the North or the terrorist

---

[86] Adam Thiam, "Au coeur du dispositif antiterroriste d'ATT: Le Pspdn et ses hommes,"
Sahara Medias FR, July 30, 2010.

[87] Interview with Berabiche leader, Bamako, Mali, October 4, 2013; Eric Wulf and Farley
Mesko, *Guide to a Post-Conflict Mali*, Washington, D.C.: C4ADS, 2013, p. 15; International
Crisis Group, *Avoiding Escalation*, Africa Report No. 189, Brussels, July 18, 2012, pp. 6–7.

threat. There was a high-level effort by President Ibrahim Boubacar Keïta following his election in fall 2013 to develop, if not a full national security strategy, at least a strategic plan for moving Mali's security forces forward. Much of this effort took place in the context of the drafting of a Military Orientation and Planning Law (Loi d'orientation et de programmation militaire, LOPM)—roughly equivalent to the U.S. Quadrennial Defense Review. This effort, however, stalled, and Bamako did not pass the LPM until February 2015.

The Malian officers interviewed for this study left little doubt about their propensity to regard the CAGs as posing the more pressing security problem, notwithstanding the peace process. Indeed, they appear to resent the international community for insisting on what they regard as a largely artificial distinction between the rebels and the jihadists. For example, a senior army military intelligence officer interviewed for this study observed that there has to be a comprehensive strategy, but "the political process, the international community, and the French make things difficult" by, among other things, insisting on a difference between the CAGs and the terrorist groups.[88] As discussed above, several of the officers interviewed for this study, including the senior army intelligence officer, held the conviction that the CAGs and terrorist groups are more or less one and the same.[89] When asked about a Malian CT strategy, they did no more than point to the ongoing negotiations and express the hope that peace negotiations and a resulting peace accord would clear the air by "separating the good potatoes from the bad," revealing which groups really were serious about reaching political accommodations with the Malian state and which were not.[90] For the CAGs that turned out to be "good," the plan, according to one officer, was to convince the international community to help Mali meet its needs.[91] Otherwise, most of those interviewed seemed to

---

[88] Interview with senior FAMa intelligence officer, Bamako, Mali, January 19, 2015.

[89] Interview with senior FAMa intelligence officer, Bamako, Mali, January 19, 2015; interview with senior Gendarmerie nationale officer, Bamako, Mali, January 23, 2015.

[90] Interview with senior FAMa intelligence officer, Bamako, Mali, January 19, 2015; interview with Malian general officer, Bamako, Mali, January 22, 2015.

[91] Interview with Malian general officer, Bamako, Mali, January 22, 2015.

see little good coming out of a peace accord itself. For example, according to a senior Gendarmerie nationale commander, even if a deal were signed, it would not be sincere because it would result from outside (international) pressure. The same Gendarmerie officer speculated that the CAGs would learn to fine-tune their activities so that they avoid doing anything so dramatic as to force France or the United States to reconsider the CAGs' status as "good faith" signatories and categorize them as terrorist groups.[92]

With respect to developing an appropriate doctrine and strategy, Malians face two main challenges, according to one officer: First, senior Malian officers have received a patchwork of training from U.S., French, Soviet, and other sources. Second, Malian commanders and planners have to move beyond thinking about conventional military capabilities and requirements ("We are not going to war against Burkina Faso any more") and focus entirely on the internal security mission and the requirements of asymmetrical warfare ("Using tanks to defend Gao doesn't work").[93]

These statements reflect an appreciation for the particularities of Sahelian warfare, which generally privileges maneuver and speed, as well as vehicles with light sustainment requirements. There is more: The officers interviewed for this study evinced some understanding of the need for a military approach that was more comprehensive in the sense of being less focused on fighting and tactics and more attentive to public opinion and building relations between the military and the state, on one side, and the people, on the other. This vision is consistent with the U.S. doctrine on COIN and stability operations (although the United States itself has not been promoting COIN or stability operations doctrine in Mali). For example, several officers cited the importance of "hearts and minds" operations (such as Medical Civic Action Programs), designed to provide services, which they acknowledge the Malian state is not providing. These officers also want to foster positive

---

[92] Interview with senior Gendarmerie nationale anti-terrorism officer, Bamako, Mali, January 23, 2015.

[93] Interview with Malian general officer, Bamako, Mali, January 22, 2015.

interactions between the troops and civilians.[94] Economic development and education are other needs.[95] One officer acknowledged that Mali was doing such a poor job of providing services that locals were "better off" when MUJAO was in control.[96] Several indicated an appreciation for working with the population and conducting influence operations, although, according to a senior army intelligence officer, the army itself is focused on more-conventional "security" operations.[97]

A senior officer articulated a particularly comprehensive vision of what Mali needed to do to prevail. First, he argued that Mali needed a "republican" army. He offered criteria for this army:

1. It does not do coups d'état, it has a clear hierarchy, and it is subordinate to civilian authority. It should have a culture in which officers know that they are there to serve the politicians and not make policy.
2. The army acts within a legal and social normative framework, in which everyone involved understands that they are individually responsible.
3. The army respects the other institutions of the republic.
4. It exists to propagate democracy and the republic and is at the service of the citizens.[98]

The idea of making the FAMa more republican speaks to the realization that the FAMa and Mali's other security services often fall short with respect to such matters as rule of law and human rights, especially in the North; moreover, it also speaks to an awareness of the military's

---

[94] Interview with regional FAMa and Gendarmerie nationale senior officers, Timbuktu, Mali, January 20, 2014; interview with senior FAMa intelligence officer, Bamako, Mali, January 19, 2015.

[95] Interview with regional FAMa and Gendarmerie nationale senior officers, Timbuktu, Mali, January 20, 2014; interview with senior FAMa intelligence officer, Bamako, Mali, January 19, 2015.

[96] Interview with senior Gendarmerie nationale officer, Bamako, Mali, January 23, 2015.

[97] Interview with regional FAMa senior officer, Timbuktu, Mali, January 20, 2015; interview with senior FAMa intelligence officer, Bamako, Mali, January 19, 2015.

[98] Interview with Malian general officer, Bamako, Mali, January 22, 2015.

often-antagonistic relationship with northerners, many of whom are likely to regard the FAMa as a foreign force that generates insecurity rather than providing security. In effect, the FAMa's inability to operate successfully in the North and create security arguably has at least as much to do with its comportment and relations with northern minorities as it does with the military's strictly operational capabilities. As we will discuss, we saw little evidence that Mali's security services or its international partners (EUTM) were providing more than nominal assistance with respect to making the FAMa more republican.

In addition, the same officer argued for taking a set of concomitant steps:

1. Address religious radicalization through a series of measures, including fostering a religious dialogue to communicate "a better view of Islam," a strategic communication effort; monitoring preaching and the foreign financing of Muslim groups and organizations; and the implementation in Mali of the deradicalization effort that has yielded impressive results in Mauritania.
2. Control Mali's frontiers and establish a surveillance network.
3. Control key locations, such as water points in Saharan mountain formations, which rebels and traffickers use to take shelter. The French sweep these sites but lack the ability to monitor them continuously.
4. Build a special forces capability.[99]

The officer's insistence on a Special Forces capability is indicative of the value that Malian leaders appear to place on having a strong Special Forces capability, which they regard as something they lost in the wake of the 2012 coup, with the dissolution of the 33e RCP. Indeed, the army is determined to push ahead with forming a new battalion-sized special operations unit. There is no mention of the unit in the defense law, and it is unclear what precisely the new force is intended to accomplish, what its doctrine will be, or what its reporting chain will look like, though it will be "short," perhaps going through

---

[99] Interview with Malian general officer, Bamako, Mali, January 22, 2015.

the chief of the general staff and defense minister to the president.[100] Several interviewees underlined the limits of conventional units. One expressed frustration with existing conventional units that cannot do precision operations, are not discreet or mobile, and are too costly.[101] Another interviewee indicated that they lack the ability to endure in remote areas and to fight aggressively against terrorists.[102] The army has already begun selection efforts to fill the new Special Forces unit's ranks, with the goal of pulling into the new battalion roughly 10 percent of the existing army; the efforts so far appear to be focused on general physical fitness and mental health.[103]

In any case, the Malians' use of the term *Special Forces* should not create the impression that the FAMa are interested in either high-end, commando-type operations or sophisticated COIN work. Ultimately, what the FAMa want is an arm that is competent, capable of aggressive offensive operations, and small enough to be manageable. In the end, the new battalion presents a dilemma for U.S. security cooperation efforts. Should the United States work to develop this new force, recognizing that the Malians have an unusually strong commitment to the concept, or should it focus on the broader force, and on basic capacity building, rather than the advanced techniques of a special unit?

Investing in a new Special Forces capability is not without risk. Our interviews with Malian officers suggest that this choice may reflect disinterest in or perhaps pessimism on the part of Malian commanders, with respect to raising the overall effectiveness of the rest of the force. The temptation is strong, then, to take the seemingly easier route of building a new capability associated with new units rather than do the hard work of thinking about what kind of force structure Mali needs and then restructuring the existing force accordingly—a potentially painful and politically costly exercise that probably would

---

[100] Interview with senior FAMa Special Forces battalion officer, Bamako, Mali, January 22, 2015.

[101] Interview with senior FAMa Special Forces battalion officer, Bamako, Mali, January 22, 2015.

[102] Interview with Malian general officer, Bamako, Mali, January 22, 2015.

[103] Interview with senior Special Forces battalion officer, Bamako, Mali, January 22, 2015.

involve abandoning certain capabilities and disbanding certain units. Moreover, for a military that has difficulty controlling its people and equipment spread across a number of locations, and deployed to remote areas, neglecting the bulk of the force in favor of concentrating on a subset consisting of the top 10 percent of the army must appear very tempting. "It seems self-evident that one would focus first on regular forces before turning to Special Forces," an EUTM officer observed, "but the Malians clearly are fixated on [Special Forces]."[104] Finally, the FAMa's focus on acquiring, quickly, a SOF capability as they understand it also speaks to another problem: However much Malian military leaders refer to the need to adopt a broader, more COIN- or stability operations–like approach to dealing with northerners or to build a republican force, they continue to default to a focus on tactical and offensive military capabilities. Illustrative of Mali's approach, despite the awareness of some Malian leaders of the need to back away from purely tactical military solutions, is the May 2014 attempt by the Malian Army to seize Kidal, which at the time was controlled by several CAGs, chief among them the MNLA. The assault, which Bamako mounted using primarily EUTM-trained units, bears all the hallmarks of haste, and it resulted in a debacle. Setting aside the operational failures, which included an apparent inability to coordinate, as well as logistical problems, the French defense analyst Laurent Touchard noted what the catastrophe said about Bamako's strategic thinking, or lack thereof:

> To retake Kidal without the "materials" required to provide for the daily life and security of the local population, without viable projects for the nomadic communities, without ensuring the protection of human rights, is to put the plow before the oxen without having oxen. On the contrary, if Bamako wanted to sow the seeds of an umpteenth Tuareg rebellion, well, this is a good way to go about it.[105]

---

[104]Interview with EUTM officers, Bamako, Mali, January 30, 2015.

[105]Laurent Touchard, "CONOPS: Décryptage: Paris–Bamako, je t'aime, moi non plus," *CONOPS*, June 8, 2013b.

The Malian focus on offensive military operations, notwithstanding some awareness of the need for a broader approach called for by COIN or stability operations doctrine, also highlights the fact that the Malian approach has not differed substantially from that promoted by Mali's partners—i.e., France and the United States. While Mali and its partners have different assessments of the nature of the threat, all have focused on offensive operations, tactics, and the associated capabilities. This suggests that there might be room for France and the United States to shift their own focus with regard to what they tell the Malians regarding how to deal with threats in the North.

The Turn to Militias

The failure at Kidal and Bamako's impatience with regard to the army's progress prompted the government soon after Kidal to play the same card it used in the 1990s to redress the military balance of power in the North: Bamako tapped ethnic militias and tasked them not with targeting jihadist groups but, on the contrary, with doing what the FAMa could not do—matching the CAGs on the battlefield—at the risk of creating long-term political and security problems for the sake of short-term gain. The Malian government plainly has not learned from the experience of the 1990s, when the Songhay militia it sponsored, the Ganda Koy, targeted Arab and Tuareg communities, precipitating the worst bloodshed by far in that decade and doing significant damage to intercommunal relations and relations between the government and many of the North's communities.[106]

The two most important pro-government militias today are the GATIA and MAA-Platform. GATIA, led by now-General El Hadj Ag Gamou, appears to consist primarily of Tuaregs from the Imghad caste, who historically have been at odds with the Tuareg elite castes

---

[106]Baz Lecocq describes the Gonda Koy as having been founded and led by ostensibly deserted Malian Army officers who continued to wear their uniforms and who enjoyed at least tacit support from the military. See Baz Lecocq, *That Desert Is Our Country: Tuareg Rebellions and Competing Nationalisms in Contemporary Mali (1946–1996)*, Amsterdam: Academisch Proefschrift, 2002, p. 272.

associated today with the HCUA and the MNLA.[107] It was Gamou and his fighters who accompanied Serval forces as they advanced into northern Mali.[108] As for MAA-Platform, the former Arab rebel leader Mohamed Ould Meydou leads it. Meydou, like Gamou, joined the army after the rebellion of the 1990s, and in 2008 he led an Arab militia alongside Gamou's Imghad to put down the Tuareg rebellion. He is now a FAMa general.

GATIA and MAA-Platform officially have nothing to do with the Malian government, although it is widely assumed that Bamako supports them. Gamou and Meydou, for example, remain in uniform. Moreover, the January 2015 issue of the FAMa magazine *Le Guido*, which was distributed to foreign military officers who attended the Army Day ceremony, includes a full-page laudatory profile of GATIA. The article singles out the Imghad as the only Tuareg who loyally defended Mali.[109] This assertion, aside from being factually inaccurate, can only reinforce and give credence to suspicions that Bamako is uninterested in representing all of Mali's people and has taken sides in some ethnic communities' conflicts with others.

GATIA and MAA-Platform stand out for several reasons. First, they clearly are more effective than the FAMa, although the reasons for this, besides their greater comfort with operating in the North, are unclear. They might, for example, use tactics better suited for the terrain and indigenous capabilities than those the FAMa use. Second, both have been implicated in trafficking, and indeed clashes between them and the CAGs may have less to do with politics than with economic interests and the desire to control trafficking points.[110] Third,

---

[107] Gamou led the Imghads in battle against the Tuareg elites in the 1990s, and, after integrating into the Malian Army, led an Imghad militia against Tuareg rebels in 2008. See Boilley, 1999, p. 515; Grémont, 2010, p. 21; and Lecocq, 2010, pp. 400–401.

[108] "Les touaregs du Col. Ag Gamou et l'armée française aux portes de Tessalit," video, posted to YouTube by ImazighenLibya, February 9, 2013.

[109] Ahmadou Maiga, "Pourquoi le Gatia?" *Le Guido*, January 2015, p. 20.

[110] Interview with a Western European officer attached to MINUSMA, Bamako, January 26, 2015. See also United Nations Security Council, 2014b, p. 2; "UN Holds Talks to Calm North Mali Town as Armed Groups Clash," *Voice of America*, January 19, 2015.

Mali's collaboration with specific subsets of specific ethnic communities, such as the Imghad Tuareg, belies official discourses prioritizing unity and undermines attempts to reach out to northern communities, convince them of the government's good will, and generate support among them. At the very least, favoring the Imghad does Bamako no favors among the elite aristocratic Tuareg tribes who might feel threatened by the upstart commoners, other Tuaregs who simply might disapprove of their appropriation of power, and any community that regards itself as competing with the Imghads economically or otherwise.

Finally, it should be added that the pro-Bamako militias, MAA-Platform and GATIA, cannot be reduced to proxy forces wholly controlled by the Malian state.[111] The Arab and Tuareg militias may advance Bamako's agenda vis-à-vis the rebel groups, but they also represent the interests of particular groups involved in local conflicts. The opposition between the MNLA and GATIA, for example, is grounded in an intracommunal fight pitting rival Tuareg fractions against one another. Groups appeared to be fighting in a show of force with the Algiers process as a background, but there likely was an economic motive: The United Nations has highlighted "competition for the control of strategic commercial and trafficking routes" as a key factor behind clashes between armed groups, which tend to be localized around key crossing points or other areas of strategic interest for the circulation of licit and illicit goods.[112]

Conclusion

Mali after Serval is an increasingly dangerous place, notwithstanding ongoing French combat operations, MINUSMA, and the Algiers Accords, which establish a framework for deescalating northern Mali's various conflicts. Mali's terrorist groups are increasingly active and expanding the geographic range of their operations; they also appear to be enjoying some popular support and clearly have taken root in Mali,

---

[111] International Crisis Group, 2015, p. 5.

[112] United Nations Security Council, 2015, para. 16.

as opposed to constituting a foreign presence. Moreover, the terrorist problem is clearly deeply entangled in northern Mali's larger security issues, both because of ties between and among terrorist and non-jihadi rebel groups—the signatories of the Algiers Accords—and because of the relevance of various overlapping drivers.

The Algiers Accords represent a necessary step forward, but the agreement is far from sufficient either to bring peace to northern Mali or to achieve an objective sought by Mali's international partners—namely, to more or less settle the political conflicts so that Mali and its partners can focus on the terrorist threat. Such a view overlooks the profound interconnectedness of the terrorist and political problems; the fact that the agreement does little to address the drivers of the conflict (of which the North's relationship with the South is but one); and the military imbalance between North and South, more specifically between the CAGs and the FAMa. Lastly, many Malians themselves tend not to distinguish between the terrorists and the CAGs, which they regard as a greater threat than the terrorists.

Mali's military is aware of the need for a broader set of capabilities in line with COIN or stability operations, instead of simple tactical and offensive fire and maneuver capabilities. The FAMa need to work on relations with the North's inhabitants, provide services, and otherwise do what they can to build legitimacy. Among other things, they have to become more "republican" and integrate northern minorities more effectively. That said, the army's attempt to take Kidal in 2014, the FAMa's current interest in acquiring a SOF capability as they understand it, and the FAMa's use of ethnic militias betray a focus on addressing the military balance in the North vis-à-vis the CAGs and a tendency—similarly embraced by a number of Mali's international partners, including the United States—to default to focusing on fighting as a sufficient solution to Mali's problems.

CHAPTER FOUR
Mali's Capabilities and Limitations

Mali's security services face serious gaps in capabilities and systemic problems that make them a low-capability partner for the international community in the short term and unlikely to become fully independent of outside aid in the medium to long term. While this report notes several areas where the acquisition of new capabilities would be useful, entrenched problems of institutional culture and poor leadership on the part of many mid- and senior-ranking officers make achieving lasting gains in capabilities quite difficult. This chapter focuses primarily on the army, although we also highlight certain attributes of the Gendarmerie and Garde. We used DSART, developed by RAND for the Department of Defense and commonly used by U.S. civilian federal agencies and civil society organizations specializing in security sector reform, as a reference, although we did not apply the tool formally.[1] We also went beyond DSART to focus first on a number of the Malian security forces' broader problems, including their failures vis-à-vis the integration of ethnic minorities and their fraught relationship with northern populations.

Overall, the FAMa would benefit from becoming better at relating appropriately with northern populations and fostering state legitimacy, through a variety of means—hence becoming a truly republican army. Such means include civic outreach and humanitarian activities, as well as the recruitment and improved integration of members of northern minorities. With regard to more-classic military capabilities,

---

[1] Agnes G. Schaefer and Lynn E. Davis, *Defense Sector Assessment Rating Tool*, Santa Monica, Calif.: RAND Corporation, TR-864-OSD, 2010.

the FAMa's poor ability to carry out basic functions suggest that a "slow and steady wins the race" approach to getting to the level of capability it seeks would be most prudent. This means focusing on basic skills and acquiring capabilities and equipment that are easy to use and easy to maintain.

"Republican" Culture and Failed Integration

It is not an exaggeration to claim that Mali's security forces—above all, the army—can be more effective at antagonizing northern populations than combating the CAGs and jihadist groups, and, consequently, they often represent a net loss for Mali with respect to security and government legitimacy. From this point of view, changing the balance with respect to the military's contribution to security and legitimacy has as much to do with improving its beliefs and comportment as it does strengthening its military capabilities vis-à-vis, say, AQIM.

As discussed in Chapter Two, the southern-dominated Malian Army historically has related to northern Mali as a quasi-foreign land,[2] and northerners have regarded the army as a foreign army of occupation.[3] Malian Army leadership, moreover, made no effort to bridge the gap between its troops and northern populations by conducting any sort of instruction or training that might have informed the troops about the North or taught northerners about the South and about army members.[4]

Prior to 1993, the army recruited few Tuaregs, and most of them served in the Gardes Nomades, an irregular camel corps that dated to the French colonization.[5] Those Tuaregs who served in the army had

---

[2] This, however, does not diminish in any way the attachment of the average Malian (in the South but also, to a large extent, in the North) to the territorial integrity of the country. Support for an independent North remains confined to specific (and small) subgroups of the population.

[3] Mariko, 2001, p. 48.

[4] Mariko, 2001, p. 52.

[5] Grémont, 2010, p. 12.

little hope of promotion: the Mali expert Charles Grémont writes that, to his knowledge, only two or three Tuaregs became officers between 1960 and 1993. Most of the Tuaregs in the army deserted with the outbreak of rebellion in 1991.[6]

According to Grémont, 1993 brought about a shift in the history of Arab and Tuareg recruitment in the army, as well as Mali's other security forces. Peace negotiations yielded a disarmament, demobilization, and reintegration (DDR) program that involved the integration of Arab and Tuareg rebel fighters into Mali's security forces, the army among them. The first batch joined the ranks in 1993; there would be several others subsequently, with the total reaching "more than 2,500" in 1996 (out of a total force that was unlikely to have been greater than 15,000).[7] More came between 2006 and 2009, as a result of the rebellion of those years. The FAMa also began recruiting directly from Arab and Tuareg communities, although we have not been able to come up with any numbers.

As discussed, large numbers of these Tuareg fighters along with their Arab peers deserted the force in 2012. The reasons for the failure to effectively integrate these men into the force are multiple. One is a lack of confidence in the Malian state, as well as a sense that, ultimately, southern Malians do not regard the North as part of their country. For example, an Arab colonel who deserted and then joined an Arab armed group said that Mali's abandonment of the North in 2012 signaled to him that Mali did not care enough about the North to defend it, and that ultimately his community was on its own. He said, moreover, that even though his career as a FAMa officer went well and he was never mistreated, the southerners never let him forget that he was different.[8] A number of the officers interviewed for this study voiced a recognition of the importance of getting right the integration of soldiers from the North, both new recruits and former rebel fighters who had been integrated in the past into Mali's security forces as part of past peace accords and who are likely to return as part of a future

---

[6] Grémont, 2010, p. 14.

[7] Grémont, 2010, p. 18.

[8] Interview with MAA colonel, Bamako, Mali, October 8, 2013.

peace deal.[9] They acknowledged that past efforts at integrating former rebels had largely failed because, among other reasons, there was never a policy in place regarding how to integrate them, and in the absence of a policy, nothing really was done to smooth the transition from rebel fighter to Malian soldier and integrate the soldiers into cohesive units. In the words of a Malian officer, "reintegration must be done more carefully."[10] According to one Gendarmerie nationale commander, "We thought it was sufficient to give them a uniform and some money, and a little training. It wasn't enough. . . . The point was to create citizenship, but we didn't do that. We need to form them in citizenship."[11]

The gendarmes estimate that 30 percent of the reintegrated forces in their ranks left the force again.[12] In part, according to the commander, this is because reintegration efforts allowed rebel commanders to preserve their hierarchies by establishing a rank structure based on the hierarchies of rebel units.[13] In addition, in the rush to reintegrate combatants following the peace agreement, the gendarmes, as well as Mali's other security services, overlooked basic thresholds for education and failed to teach fighters concepts of citizenship; together these meant that fighters would neither feel loyal nor confident on the job, and the population would not trust these new recruits.[14]

As for recruiting Arabs and Tuaregs generally, old habits appear to persist. One officer who noted that the army needed to recruit more northerners said that presently the army relies on Imghad Tuaregs.[15] It is not clear whether he or other Malian military leaders are aware of or concerned about the implications of associating Mali's security

---

[9]   Interview with Malian general officer, Bamako, Mali, January 22, 2015; interview with senior Gendarmerie nationale officer, Bamako, Mali, January 23, 2015; interview with senior FAMa Special Forces battalion officer, Bamako, Mali, January 22, 2015.

[10]   Interview with Malian general officer, Bamako, Mali, January 22, 2015.

[11]   Interview with senior Gendarmerie nationale officer, Bamako, Mali, January 23, 2015.

[12]   Interview with senior Gendarmerie nationale officer, Bamako, Mali, January 23, 2015.

[13]   Interview with senior Gendarmerie nationale officer, Bamako, Mali, January 23, 2015.

[14]   Interview with Malian general officer, Bamako, Mali, January 22, 2015; interview with senior Gendarmerie nationale officer, Bamako, Mali, January 23, 2015.

[15]   Interview with Malian general officer, Bamako, Mali, January 22, 2015.

services with a particular northern community, especially one that is at odds with other northern communities. Recruiting Imghad Tuaregs enhances the FAMa's capabilities; recruiting only Imghads, however, is likely to be counterproductive because it antagonizes other communities and associates Bamako with Imghad interests.

With the stakes so high, Mali should begin to plan now for an eventual reintegration of CAGs. Indeed, Chapter Eight of the Algiers Accords calls for DDR and the integration of "eligible combatants." Attention should be paid to providing basic education and citizenship classes for these recruits and using outcomes of this training to drive placement of these recruits within the armed forces. Next, the Malian armed forces should be aware of the rank structures of the CAGs and ensure that, while seniority is considered, rebel units are not replicated inside the FAMa.

More must be done to narrow the distance between the army and northern populations. More diversity would certainly help, as would a host of other improvements, including better compliance with human rights laws and basic efforts to build mutual familiarity. As a Western European officer in MINUSMA put it, politically, the FAMa need to have a presence in the North, but they are not well received, and they tend to generate aggression rather than security.[16] A 2015 report by the human rights organization CIVIC notes from its interviews on the ground that "few civilians in northern Mali perceive the FAMa as a credible or effective security actor in the North."[17] Yet, and somewhat paradoxically, "many interviewees wished to see a continued or expanded FAMa presence, and, in some cases, asked that the FAMa receive more training on the ground."[18] The report notes that even interviewees who have been directly harmed by FAMa actions still welcome their presence more than the alternatives, which would be either a North run by militias or the security vacuum that currently

---

[16] Interview with Western European MINUSMA officer, Bamako, Mali, January 26, 2015.

[17] CIVIC, 2015, p. 34.

[18] CIVIC, 2015, p. 34.

exists in many areas.[19] This suggests that the population is hopeful that a more effective, inclusive, and accountable FAMa can become the security provider (or one of the security providers) that people need in the North.

Composition of the Military

Mali's armed forces technically include the army, air force, Gendarmerie nationale, Garde nationale, and Police nationale, although colloquially the term *FAMa* often refers more exclusively to the army and air force, or sometimes just the army, in recognition of its external security role versus the internal role of the other services. As a landlocked country, Mali does not have an independent navy but maintains a riverine capability, consisting of roughly three patrol boats.[20]

The size of Mali's armed forces is often cited as about 15,600 strong, using a figure from *Military Balance* or *Jane's*.[21] However, some dispute this figure and calculate it to be as high as 26,000.[22] In point of fact, the total number of service members in the FAMa is unknown; EUTM is in the process of completing a database of soldiers, funded by the Canadian government, known as the Human Resources Information System (Système d'information des ressources humaines, SIRH) that will allow the military to keep track of size, as well as a number of other factors.[23]

The Malian Army follows a similar rank structure as the French, which is itself similar to the U.S. structure. While salary data were not

---

[19] CIVIC, 2015, p. 34.

[20] International Institute for Strategic Studies, "Chapter Nine: Sub-Saharan Africa," *The Military Balance*, Vol. 115, No. 1, 2015, p. 443.

[21] "Mali—Armed Forces," Jane's Sentinel Security Assessment—North Africa, *Jane's Defence*, October 14, 2014; International Institute for Strategic Studies, 2015, pp. 443–444.

[22] Laurent Touchard, "CONOPS: Revue de détails; Les forces armées maliennes de Janvier 2012 à Janvier 2013," *CONOPS*, January 15, 2013a.

[23] "Les forces armées maliennes se dotent d'un système d'information pour la gestion de leurs effectifs," European Union Training Mission in Mali, January 23, 2014.

obtained for this study, one Malian Army officer did note that soldiers receive 50,000 CFA francs (approximately $83) per month in bonus pay for serving in the northern regions.

Out of all of Mali's security forces, the Gendarmerie has the highest required level of educational attainment to qualify for service, compared with the army, the Garde nationale, and the Police nationale. All of Mali's uniformed services, however, face serious shortages in terms of human capital, based on low levels of educational attainment at the national level. For example, in 2013, the World Bank estimated the youth literacy rate at 47 percent and adult literacy rate at 34 percent.[24] As with the overall staffing levels, there are no data available on the breakdown of ethnicities in the military. However, by reputation, the Garde is thought to contain the highest numbers of northern minorities, because of the fact that units are formed locally across the country. A number of northern minority fighters were also integrated into the FAMa following the 1992 peace agreement. Many have since left the military, but a significant portion remains. We were unable to obtain precise data regarding who left and who stayed behind. According to one source, the motives of those who deserted varied depending on the individual.[25] Some defected to rebel groups; others left simply to seek safety or look after their families.

Military Organization

The Malian military is garrisoned based on eight regional divisions and has a mix of infantry, armored, artillery, and engineering units. At the institutional level, it is organized under the president, who also serves as commander-in-chief of the armed forces. The Ministry of Defense and Veterans' Affairs is led by a civilian minister, Tiéman Hubert Coulibaly. He was appointed in January 2015, following a cabinet shuffle that saw a number of officials replaced in an attempt by the president to improve the image of the government and make it more responsive to the population's concerns. The chief of the general staff, Major General Mahamane Touré, was put into place in November 2013, fol-

---

[24] World Bank, "World Development Indicators," *World DataBank*, April 14, 2015.

[25] Interview with Tuareg community member, Bamako, Mali, January 23, 2015.

lowing the army coup that year, and though he tendered his resignation after an incident in which a soldier opened fire on the president's car, he was kept in position.[26] Despite the titular civilian leadership of the ministry, Touré is a powerful actor in the formulation of defense policy. Under the office of the chief of the general staff, there are several bureaus: operations, administration, logistics, and, according to some sources, general studies and external relations.[27]

In addition to the functional bureaus, the chief of the general staff's office sits atop the offices of the service chiefs (see Figure 4.1). While many conflate the chief of the general staff position with that of the chief of the general staff of the army, the army has its own service chief, Colonel-Major Ibrahim Fané.[28] The chief of the Gendarmes is Colonel-Major Mody Berethé, who was appointed in January 2014.

Figure 4.1
Command and Control of the Malian Armed Forces

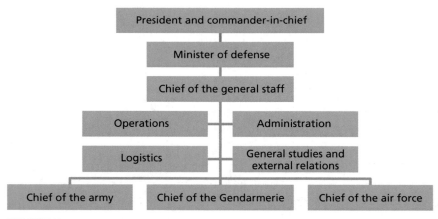

RAND RR1241-4.1

---

[26] "Mali President Replaces Junta-Linked Army Chief," *Voice of America*, November 9, 2013.

[27] Touchard, 2013; "Réforme de l'armée: La cartographie de l'organisation territoriale de la nouvelle armée du Mali," *Maliweb*, February 21, 2014.

[28] "Visite du chef d'etat major de l'armée de terre au GTIA 6," *Abamako*, January 11, 2015.

The chief of the air force is Colonel-Major Souleymane Bamba, who assumed office in May 2012.[29]

In addition to these positions, there are numerous other functions nested under the chief of the general staff authority, though the lines of authority are not always clear. These include military justice, military policing, engineering, communications, health, and social services.[30] The Malian intelligence service, Direction générale de la sécurité extérieure (Directorate-General for External Security, DGSE), does not fall under the direction of the Ministry of Defense, although it appears that the intelligence service may utilize military ranks.

Military Capabilities

Part of the problem facing the Malian Army is the disconnect between its primary requirements and what can best be described as a legacy force structure. As mentioned above, Mali's army traditionally had understood its mission to be external security, and, aided and abetted by French and Soviet security assistance programs, it pursued conventional capabilities. Mali's postcolonial leaders also understood an army to be something sovereign states have—an army was a marker of sovereignty, and what they wanted, ultimately, was an army that looked like an army, by the standards of civilians and former French Army soldiers, whose only models were first the French Army and subsequently the Soviet one. In contrast, events since 1990 and the threat analysis presented in this report indicate that the Malian Army must be prepared to confront internal security threats from deep within the desert and its mountains. In its manual on desert operations, the French Army highlights the supreme difficulty of maneuver in such hostile terrain.[31]

At the same time, the French manual points to indigenous forces' ability to maneuver quickly in coordinated thrusts—*razzias*—as the essence of Sahelian warfare, but that is something Mali's army is par-

---

[29] "Communiqué du Conseil des ministres du mercredi 16 mai 2012," *Maliweb*, May 17, 2012.

[30] Touchard, 2013a.

[31] Centre de doctrine et d'emploi des forces, 2013, p. 9.

ticularly poor at conducting.[32] Mali's security forces also have the mission of protecting the population, which obliges them to aid in the establishment of civil security in populated areas. The army plays a subordinate role in civil security, promoting public order and defending against attacks on civilians. Primary civil-order responsibilities fall to the Police nationale, though Mali's Garde nationale is tasked with the protection of vital facilities and with keeping peace and order in remote areas, and the Gendarmerie nationale engages in both rural provision of civil order and a provost function, which places it, at least on paper, in the position of being able to police the army as it conducts operations and ensure that soldiers behave appropriately among civilians.

Movement and Maneuver

Prior to the crisis, the Malian Army had four infantry battalions and two armored battalions. According to a study by the French government conducted at the outset of Operation Serval, Mali's maneuver capability of the army consisted of 35 BRDM-2 amphibious armored patrol cars, 18 BTR-60PB armored personnel carriers, and 14 T55 tanks (mostly out of service) imported from the former Soviet bloc.[33] These armored vehicles are vestiges of a time when the army thought of its mission largely in terms of external defense, in particular fighting against Mali's neighbors.[34] Mali's doctrinal references for their use, moreover, remain Soviet.

Mali has a hard time conducting coordinated maneuver. Even assuming that its armored vehicles worked, Mali's army, as the Kidal debacle exposed, does a poor job of getting different units to coordi-

---

[32] The French desert warfare manual (Centre de doctrine et d'emploi des forces, 2013) notes that the *razzia*-style of offensive strikes have a distinct advantage over static positions, which might help explain the FAMa's lack of success fending off attacks.

[33] Christophe Guilloteau and Philippe Nauche, *Rapport d'information déposé en application de l'article 145 du règlement, par la Commission de la défense nationale et des forces armées, en conclusion des travaux d'une mission d'information sur l'opération Serval au Mali*, Paris: Assemblée Nationale, Senate Report 1288, July 18, 2013.

[34] Touchard, 2013a. Touchard describes Mali's armor as a reflection of the desire to protect southern Mali, primarily from points south (i.e., Burkina Faso).

nate, and this includes EUTM battle groups (groupements tactique interarmes, GTIAs), which should by definition be able at least to organize a combined arms effort.[35] In addition, the armored vehicles, which date to the Cold War, often have not been well maintained and are ill suited to desert warfare, particularly against opponents who rely on far more maneuverable 4x4 trucks or who fight dismounted.[36] Among other things, the vehicles have no air conditioning, and the desert heat all but immobilizes their crews. The thin-skinned vehicles are no match for more quickly moving pickup trucks firing heavy machine guns or dismounted fighters with RPG-7s.[37] When asked, members of the FAMa in the northern part of the country indicated that they primarily conducted either static security or patrols, rather than mobile tactics, such as the deep attack tactics advocated by the French Army in its manual on desert warfare or used by enemy forces. Chad's army, for example, is well-known for having embraced and honed the fast pickup truck–based warfare; the Malian Army has not followed suit, although it is possible that GATIA has, which might explain why it is more effective than the FAMa.

As mines and IEDs have become a major threat, the FAMa also need to be trained and equipped accordingly. It may be useful to look at what the United Nations has been doing to increase MINUSMA's security in this regard. In late 2014, United Nations Mine Action Service (UNMAS) provided a two-month training on mines and IEDs to MINUSMA peacekeepers based in the Kidal region.[38] MINUSMA is also procuring mine-protected vehicles, including ambulances. Similar training and equipment may be necessary for Malian forces. To some extent, this is already happening. As of December 2014, UNMAS had provided explosive-hazard awareness training to more than 2,000 members of the Malian security forces, as well as specific explosive

---

[35] Laurent Touchard, "Armée malienne: Les affrontements de Kidal, chronique d'une déroute annoncée," *Jeune Afrique*, May 27, 2014b.

[36] Touchard, 2013a.

[37] Touchard, 2013a.

[38] "Kidal: Former les contingents sur le danger des mines et IED," United Nations Multidimensional Integrated Stabilization Mission in Mali, September 25, 2014.

ordnance disposal (EOD) training to 89 members.[39] The Malian Army and police will also need counter-IED equipment, which may include up-armored vehicles, EOD equipment, ground-penetrating radars, and radio-jamming devices.[40] After a fateful incident in July 2014, when a MINUSMA vehicle hit a mine near the Kidal airstrip, some protective measures were taken, including the construction of a ditch, a berm, and observation towers to prevent the further planting of mines in the area.[41] A number of Malian military facilities and strategic infrastructure may need similar work and additional surveillance. A program such as the U.S. Army Corps of Engineers Interagency and International Services may be able to assist with these needs.

Perhaps more fundamental than the problem of counter-IED training is the FAMa's apparent inability to provide Malian units with uniform sets of operable personal and crew-served rifles and machine guns, spare magazines, magazine pouches, and rifle slings.[42] Similarly, according to Major Powelson, Malians tend not to have enough linked machine gun ammunition on hand.[43] Anecdotal evidence indicates that Malian soldiers in battle in 2012 and subsequently, as soon as they deplete their one magazine or belt of machine gun ammunition, are forced to pause and repack their magazines or links.

Fires

The Malian Army has two artillery battalions and has used its fires capability in the fight against antigovernment groups in the North.[44] The army possesses 18 GRAD2M rockets, as well as M57 60-mm mor-

---

[39] "About UNMAS in Mali," United Nations Mine Action Service, December 2014.

[40] Some of the IEDs used in Mali are radio controlled (see United Nations Security Council, 2015, para. 26).

[41] Binnie, 2015.

[42] Powelson, 2013, pp. 26–27.

[43] Powelson, 2013, p. 24.

[44] "World Armies: Mali," *IHS Jane's*, October 14, 2014; "Mali Army 'Fire as Islamists Advance,'" *BBC News*, January 8, 2013.

tars, which it has been trained on by EUTM.[45] The GRAD2M rockets have a maximum range of 20 km and constitute the principal weapons of the artillery battalions. In addition, the army had eight 122-mm towed guns; however, these were unusable because of lack of maintenance and lack of towing capability.[46] Finally, the army reportedly had 60 twin-tube 23-mm submachine guns on light trucks, additional mortars (120 mm and 80 mm), and 192 pickup trucks with machine guns.[47]

The study team did not speak with any members of the army specifically responsible for fires; however, artillery remains part of the training regimen for the GTIAs, which have artillery battalions attached to them. In this context, light artillery would be a particularly useful capability, if these battle groups engage in highly mobile CT operations. On the other hand, heavy artillery is appropriate for the static security operations to defensively protect FAMa installations and the towns that surround them. In any case, the available evidence suggests that Mali's army makes poor use of its artillery, or at least those pieces that are operable, largely because of poor training, a lack of ammunition, and defective ammunition.[48]

Defensive and Static Security

When we asked soldiers deployed to the north of the country what activities they undertake on a daily basis, the answer was generally that they provide static security for their bases (and presumably parts of the surrounding areas are part of a security bubble), as well as limited patrols.[49] The deterioration of the security situation in Mali and recent attacks against FAMa positions suggest that it is imperative to secure army bases better than has been done in the past. The particu-

---

[45] "L'équipe de formateurs de la batterie d'appui feu reçoit des lance-roquettes GRAD2M," European Union Training Mission in Mali, November 5, 2013; "Le lance-roquette grad équipe EUTM Mali," *Bruxelles2*, November 6, 2013; Guilloteau and Nauche, 2013.

[46] Guilloteau and Nauche, 2013.

[47] Guilloteau and Nauche, 2013.

[48] Touchard, 2013a.

[49] Interview with FAMa officer, Timbuktu, Mali, January 20, 2015.

larly lethal attack in Nampala in January 2015—with 11 Malian soldiers killed and nine wounded—resulted from an armed group entering a Malian army base "with relative ease."[50] Army bases and depots need to be hardened to make it more difficult for rebel groups to win decisive tactical victories against army bases—victories that provide propaganda success, in addition to military equipment and supplies, and undermine the morale of Malian troops. In the case of key military facilities, measures could include additional surveillance equipment; better construction, with more obstacles (berms, trenches) put in the way of potential intruders; and stricter control of entry points and authorized personnel. To be better prepared against rocket and mortar attacks, soldiers could also be trained in counterbattery techniques.

Intelligence

The intelligence function in Mali sits under the chief of staff of the army as the G2 directorate. Lack of intelligence capabilities was a complaint we heard broadly across the Malian forces. One officer complained that the Malian forces had the ability to gather only human intelligence (HUMINT), which was a limitation.[51] He noted further that 90 percent of elements are from the South, which creates language barriers for intelligence collection. However, in Timbuktu, one officer reported receiving numerous calls a day from locals wishing to provide information on enemy movements.[52] Malian Army officers generally appeared to discount the value of HUMINT, as opposed to technical means of intelligence collection, such as signals intelligence (SIGINT) or unmanned aerial systems. This may be a by-product of international partnership efforts with countries that have advanced technical intelligence capabilities—for example, a recent intelligence training seminar hosted by the Malian government and EUTM developed a brochure

---

[50] Quoted in "Mali: L'armée attaquée près de la frontière mauritanienne, cinq morts," 2015.

[51] Interview with senior Malian military intelligence officer, Bamako, Mali, January 29, 2015.

[52] Interview with FAMa officer, Timbuktu, Mali, January 21, 2015.

for the training in which two of three photos depicted unmanned aerial systems, though these were not a subject of the training.[53]

Among the gendarmes, the understanding of intelligence value appears to be somewhat different. While gendarmes we spoke with also noted capability gaps in intelligence, they reported that every gendarme receives training to elicit information from the population and that this is made easy for them because of their role as community police in rural areas.[54] In units that deal with terrorism, one Malian gendarme reported that two to five people a day go out among the people to collect intelligence.[55]

On the issue of intelligence sharing, the army's G2 reported that general reporting goes to the minister of defense, and urgent reporting to the chief of general staff.[56] In addition, there are regular daily meetings during the week to speak with other parts of the service. While Bamako reportedly has created a national intelligence council, according to the G2, it has not met yet. Moreover, there does not appear to be robust intelligence sharing between the G2 and Mali's DGSE.

While the structure of intelligence functions prior to EUTM's intervention is unclear, the intelligence process now appears to be moving in the direction of "regional intelligence chains."[57] Aerial reconnaissance and surveillance, as well as SIGINT methods of intelligence collection, are likely to remain on the Malian wish list, though the military reports that it plans to spend only $34,000 over the next five years on dedicated intelligence and communication equipment.[58] However, advanced equipment in these areas will be exceedingly dif-

---

[53] EUTM, *Séminaire de renseignement armée de terre: Consolidation des connaissances du personnel en charge du renseignement des régions militaires et de la division renseignement de l'EMAT*, Bamako, Mali, March 11, 2015.

[54] Interview with senior Gendarmerie nationale antiterrorism officer, January 23, 2015; interview with senior Gendarmerie nationale officer, Bamako, Mali, January 23, 2015.

[55] Interview with senior Gendarmerie nationale antiterrorism officer, January 23, 2015.

[56] Interview with senior Gendarmerie nationale antiterrorism officer, January 23, 2015.

[57] EUTM, 2015.

[58] Assemblée Nationale du Mali, "Loi d'orientation et de programmation militaire," *Malijet*, February 23, 2015.

ficult for the Malian government to maintain and operate and is probably best left to international partners. Despite Mali's apparent low opinion of HUMINT, it is an essential part of CT operations. Efforts invested in training military in more-sophisticated HUMINT operations might be a more sustainable security cooperation investment.

Sustainment

In general, the sustainment functions of logistics, personnel services, and health services are managed centrally under the office of the chief of the general staff as directorates, such as the Directorate of Health Services. As described in French desert operations doctrine, the need to operate and endure in remote areas requires excellent sustainment capabilities.[59] By all accounts, these capabilities are sorely lacking across the board, and this is a linchpin issue for the armed forces. The gaps are perhaps most noticeable in the area of logistics and maintenance, as much of the equipment the FAMa have on the books is not serviceable, including most of their aircraft. The chief of the general staff described the problem in deeper terms than a lack of capability, saying that there is a need to develop a "culture of maintenance."[60] Logistics was one of the drivers of poor performance most frequently identified by both international advisers and Malian officers.[61] For example, Powelson cited as the primary reason for the inadequacy of the U.S. SOF–trained Malian Special Forces unit associated with the 33e RCP "the complete failure of the Malian logistical system to meet their [the Special Forces unit's] sustainment requirements in the harsh and remote desert environment."[62] Also disconcerting are remarks by EUTM officers to the effect that the FAMa are struggling to equip the GTIAs, which are ostensibly the pride of the army (see below), suggesting that

---

[59] Centre de doctrine et d'emploi des forces, 2013, pp. 9, 37.

[60] Interview with Malian general officer, Bamako, Mali, January 30, 2015.

[61] Interviews with members of EUTM, Bamako, Mali, January 30, 2015; members of the EUTM Advisory Task Force (ATF), Bamako, Mali, January 30, 2015; senior Gendarmerie nationale antiterrorism officer, January 23, 2015; Western European MINUSMA officer, Bamako, Mali, January 26, 2015; and senior FAMa officer, Timbuktu, Mali, January 20, 2015.

[62] Powelson, 2013, p. 54.

the situation for the rest of the army must be grave.[63] The EUTM officers also pointed to a continuing problem with corruption. Nonetheless, the advisers and officers cited above generally agreed on the need to develop logistics systems and introduce such concepts as rationing into the force. That said, several soldiers reported that supplies of gasoline were adequate; electricity was stable; and when supplies existed in Bamako, they would be sent forward to northern posts.[64]

Personnel services, such as human resources and financial management, are also areas of particular difficulty for the FAMa: There is no accurate total of the number of service members in the FAMa, creating a serious problem of "ghost soldiers," or soldiers who are on the personnel rolls but are not showing up for duty. To improve on that situation, EUTM is working to complete the SIRH. It is challenging to understand systems for promotion, salary payment, career management, and pension absent a developed human resources system. It is equally difficult to build a clear picture of how finances might affect operational sustainment. For example, some soldiers in the North commented that there were irregularities in receiving food stipends for northern deployment, but commanders noted that the soldiers had a cafeteria on base to eat in and were receiving their pay correctly. Verifying the details of financial management as they relate to operational sustainment will require additional study.

Finally, members of the EUTM ATF described health support as a problem area as well.[65] The FAMa do not have their own medical evacuation capability; instead they rely on international partners for that function. While EUTM ATF members work with the FAMa across the range of these sustainment issues, it has been difficult for them to make progress. Members of EUTM reported that while the FAMa, supported by EUTM, had been able to develop doctrine relat-

---

[63] Interview with EUTM officers, Bamako, Mali, January 30, 2015.

[64] Conversations with FAMa military aides, Timbuktu and Gao, Mali, January 20 and 21, 2015.

[65] Interview with EUTM ATF, Bamako, Mali, January 30, 2015.

ing to these varied elements of support, operationalizing these strategies has been more difficult.[66]

Command and Control

The command and control warfighting function is "the exercise of authority and direction by a properly designated commander over assigned and attached forces in the accomplishment of the mission."[67] This is a difficult capability to evaluate with precision, but there appear to be serious deficiencies of command and control within the FAMa and the army, as reported by both EUTM staff and the FAMa leadership itself.[68] The gravity of the situation is highlighted by the serious defeat in May 2014, when an army detachment of 1,000–1,200 men with light armored vehicles and artillery entered Kidal to retake the city. The Malians notified neither MINUSMA nor France of their intention to stage the attack, which President Keïta and Prime Minister Kamisese Mara subsequently denied making. The point of the offensive, as well as of an earlier visit to Kidal, was to demonstrate the government's control over the entire territory. The result was the opposite: MNLA and HCUA fighters resisted the army, inflicting heavy casualties and forcing it to retreat in disarray. Mali's army, despite EUTM training, still could not hold its own against Tuareg irregulars. Among the problems cited were poor command and control and an inability of units, which may have performed well by themselves, to coordinate operations with others.[69] Malian commanders should have understood the limitations of EUTM training, which did not prepare units for coordinated operations. To make matters worse, the attack's authors assembled a hybrid force that combined elements from EUTM units with other regular army units and El Hadj Ag Gamou's militia. Such a

---

[66] Conversation with EUTM officers, Bamako, Mali, January 30, 2015.

[67] Joint Publication 3-31, *Command and Control for Joint Land Operations*, Washington, D.C.: Joint Staff, February 24, 2014.

[68] Conversations with EUTM officers, Bamako, Mali, January 30, 2015; EUTM ATF, Bamako, Mali, January 30, 2015; and General Touré, Bamako, Mali, January 22, 2015.

[69] Laurent Touchard, "Défense: Où en sont les forces armées maliennes?" *Jeune Afrique*, June 11, 2014c.

force would have been difficult to coordinate in any situation. Finally, with regard to the Malian leaders' denial of being aware of the planned operation, it is not clear which is worse: the idea that they were in the dark or the possibility that they are unwilling to admit responsibility.

While important consideration must be given to the difficulty of exercising command and control over remote and vast terrain without easy methods of transport and communication, these deficiencies are largely because of lack of human capital in senior leadership, as well as a stovepiped command culture. In the former case, most officers have little to no education in leadership, management, and the enforcement of discipline, and in the latter, a lack of transparency and clearly conveyed intent makes orders less likely to be obeyed. In addition, the formation of different units by different countries may have helped to create a heterogeneous command culture that interferes with coordination. This is an area of continuing effort for EUTM trainers and advisers.[70] In the words of one EUTM officer: "Malian officers are all isolated from one another vertically and horizontally. They don't talk amongst themselves and in the end only do what their superior signs off on. The lower levels do not do anything."[71]

On a side note, the EU militaries represented in EUTM and, above all, the French generally are committed to mission command, which relies on entrusting lower-echelon commanders to exercise a great degree of autonomy. While they might not necessarily be attempting to teach mission command, there is clearly a disconnect between how they expect things to be done and how Malians actually conduct operations.

When faced with a terrorist threat that is becoming only more lethal, Malian armed forces need, more than ever, soldiers who are disciplined and motivated to fight. Programs that can reinforce the Malian Army's "esprit de corps," motivation, and sense of cohesion will be critical in that regard. Good leadership plays a fundamental role in creating this cohesion and motivation. Members of the EUTM Waraba battalion refused to attend their own graduation ceremony

---

[70] Guilloteau and Nauche, 2013.

[71] Interview with EUTM officers, Bamako, Mali, January 30, 2015.

because they thought that their officers had pocketed funds meant for them, which shows that suspicion against military leaders—many of whom may have reached their officer rank based on nepotism rather than merit—is a major impediment to an effective military.[72] Much of the above is contingent on appropriate training. The FAMa and EUTM do offer some training with respect to matters of rule of law, the law of war, and human rights, but much more needs to be done to create institutional cohesion.

Aviation

To conduct the types of operations required to support desert CT operations, the Malian Air Force would need to be capable of using aviation for intelligence and reconnaissance, for transport, and for attack. The air force prior to the 2012 crisis was estimated at a strength of 400 service members, with two SF-260 light attack planes from Aermacchi; one Boeing 727, four Antonov 26s, three Basler DC-3s, one Cessna 185 Skywagon, one BNG BN2, and three Cessna Skymasters for logistics; and 13 Humbert Tétras for training.[73] According to French sources, the Malians also possess four MI24 attack helicopters, as well as several outdated and inoperable MiG aircraft.[74] However, the air force today is all but grounded, because of a combination of poor pilot training and lack of maintenance. By way of an example, the one remaining Basler that could be put back into service requires expensive repairs to its wing. The Malians did not maintain the Basler after last time the United States had it repaired, and there is no indication that a culture of maintenance has developed in the air force that would justify undertaking the repair. Mali has moved forward to return to the skies, this time with a light attack capability: In June 2015, Mali signed an agreement with Brazil's Embraer to purchase six A-29 Super

---

[72] Laurent Larcher, "La révolte du premier bataillon malien formé par l'Union européenne," *La Croix*, June 14, 2013; Dorothée Thiénot, "Le blues de l'armée malienne," *Le Monde Diplomatique*, May 2013.

[73] "Mali—Air Force," *IHS Jane's*, March 16, 2015.

[74] Guilloteau and Nauche, 2013.

Tucano light attack and reconnaissance aircraft, apparently without foreign financial support.[75] This situation presents a dilemma for security cooperation efforts. The 2015 Malian LOPM gives the greatest share (about 34 percent) of defense budget over the next five years to the air force, including $342,000 in investments in aircraft.[76] This, along with the Embraer purchase, means that the Malians have sufficient interest that they are willing to invest their own money in the effort. Given the clear value of aircraft for Mali in light of its security requirements, Bamako's interest makes sense. Mali's international partners, moreover, might similarly be tempted to help the Malian Air Force at the very least restore its pre-2012 capabilities. However, security cooperation for aviation is a long-term and expensive effort. In the case of Mali, the lack of institutionalized systems to sustain both the craft and training make this a risky investment.

Unique Gendarmerie Nationale and Garde Nationale Capabilities
The Gendarmerie nationale and Garde nationale present their own problems; however, they also bring to the table certain strengths that in some regards arguably make them more capable than the army with respect to CT and at the very least make them essential to the CT effort. The Gendarmerie nationale is a paramilitary force that shares internal security duties with the Police nationale, with the former having a greater role in rural Mali, while the latter focuses on Malian towns. The Garde nationale is a legacy of the colonial era: It is a direct descendant of the internal security forces created by French colonial authorities and recruited from local communities, especially northern communities, to maintain public order, enforce tax collection, and patrol Mali's long borders and vast deserts.[77]

Perhaps Gendarmerie nationale's and Garde nationale's most important quality is the greater confidence they appear to generate

---

[75] Aaron Mehta, "Super Tucano Nets Sale to Mali," *DefenseNews*, June 15, 2015.

[76] Assemblée Nationale du Mali, 2015.

[77] "La garde nationale du Mali," Facebook post by Vive L'Armée Républicaine du Mali, January 8, 2013.

among the population relative to the army: The anecdotal evidence indicates that the Gendarmerie and the Garde have a significantly better relationship with northern communities than the army does, and northerners are more likely to trust the Gendarmerie and the Garde than the army. One reason is that the Gendarmerie and Garde have always counted among their ranks a higher proportion of northern minorities. Indeed, according to a senior army Special Forces battalion officer, his unit and the army in general have a relatively hard time recruiting northerners because they are more comfortable with the Garde.[78] Another reason is that their very functions oblige them to operate with and among Malian civilians. They are more likely to understand the northern communities and more likely to interact with them in an appropriate manner. As a senior Gendarmerie CT officer put it, "Our advantage, it's our close policing. . . . We are in permanent contact with the population and their traditional leaders [*chefferies*]."[79]

Another thing that makes the Gendarmerie distinct from the army and particularly valuable is its *prévôtal* role. This role, best translated in English as a *provost* or *provost marshal–type* function, places gendarmes in the field alongside the military to ensure that soldiers act within the limits of the law. Malian gendarmes have the theoretical ability to cite and arrest Malian soldiers in the field for violating citizens' rights. Our interviewees have indicated that Gendarmerie personnel do in fact accompany army patrols; however, the available evidence suggests that their capacity to play the *prévôtal* role officially assigned to them—and the capacity of the general civil and military justice system to back them up and follow through with any official measures that Gendarmerie officers might take against army personnel—is minimal. This in and of itself represents a potentially valuable opportunity for Mali's international partners to focus capacity-building resources.

---

[78] Interview with senior FAMa Special Forces battalion officer, Bamako, Mali, January 22, 2015.

[79] Interview with senior Gendarmerie nationale CT officer, Bamako, Mali, January 23, 2015.

The Gendarmerie's Special Forces

The Gendarmerie boasts a Special Forces unit that merits highlighting because of the CT role given to it and for its apparently high degree of professionalism. The unit is known as the Peloton d'intervention de la Gendarmerie nationale (PIGN; National Gendarmerie Intervention Platoon), a 120-person squadron with three officers, created in 2006. The unit is tasked with operations relating to terrorism; banditry; hostage situations; and the escort of officials, detainee escort, and special security for embassies (see Figure 4.2).[80] In addition, because of the special intelligence requirements of many of its missions (such as hostage rescue), PIGN conducts its own intelligence collection.[81] While it

Figure 4.2
PIGN Vehicle Staging

SOURCE: Photograph taken by
S. Rebecca Zimmerman.
RAND RR1241-4.2

---

[80] Interview with PIGN officer, Bamako, Mali, January 23, 2015.

[81] Interview with PIGN officer, Bamako, Mali, January 23, 2015.

is in theory able to respond anywhere in the country, in practice, its response is limited to Bamako and environs, and the unit can respond within 15 minutes to an attack in the center of town.[82] In January 2015, PIGN conducted 18 missions.[83] PIGN has a short but confusing chain of command; for routine matters, it sits under a ministerial special unit immediately under the chief of the Gendarmerie. However, in an emergency, the operational command element, the ministerial special unit, or the chief may task the unit. One interesting characteristic of the unit is that numerous international partners, from French to Egyptians, have trained it. However, it still lacks several capabilities that the Gendarmerie would like to make it capable in, such as EOD, counter-IED operations, and canine operations.[84]

Persistent Patrol and the Camel Concept of Operations

The Garde also conducts a broad category of operations that is critical for both CT and civilian-military relations: long-range and long-duration patrolling out in the desert among nomads, usually by troops recruited from the same milieu. In the colonial era, this work was done by *goumiers*, or Gardes nomades, who were camel-mounted Arab and Tuareg irregulars charged with policing the wastelands that French regulars and their indigenously recruited infantry—the Tirailleurs Sénégalais—could not possibly cover. The *goumiers* could travel great distances for long periods because they knew the terrain (and its watering spots) and knew the inhabitants, with whom they regularly interacted. Today's version is more likely to be equipped with Toyota pickup trucks (although the Garde still has six camel units, according to its website); however, the concept of operations remains essentially the same. The advantages of this kind of operation for CT are self-evident, and it is clear that Mali's security forces would benefit from more of this capability. Indeed, three of our interviewees noted the value of the old *goumier*-style operations and stated that they should have more

---

[82] Interview with PIGN officer, Bamako, Mali, January 23, 2015.

[83] Interview with PIGN officer, Bamako, Mali, January 23, 2015.

[84] Interview with senior Gendarmerie nationale officer, Bamako, Mali, January 23, 2015; interview with PIGN officer, Bamako, Mali, January 23, 2015.

of that capability, but they have written off using actual camels for combat operations largely because of their slow speed relative to pick-ups and motorcycles.[85] Mali's army does not possess this kind of capability, which army leaders appear to identify as something they would like to see their Special Forces undertake.[86]

Conduct of Defense Policy

Mali has several key policy reforms in process that affect the conduct of the military; however, it was very difficult to obtain an up-to-date understanding of where these proposed policies were. The first of these is a massive security sector reform effort undertaken by the Malian government for the purpose of proposing structural reforms to the security sector. This effort, begun in 2013, has not yet resulted in a formal proposal or bill brought before the legislature. The key bill that has been adopted by the National Assembly so far is the Malian Military Planning Law, which sets forth a new vision and top-level budget needs for the FAMa for the next five years.

Executive and Legislature

The Malian military has a historically close relationship with the office of the president of Mali, on whose power there are relatively few checks. The president is both the commander-in-chief and the head of defense policy; he appoints both the minister of defense and the chief of the defense staff. In theory, the legislature has the ability to provide oversight of the executive branch, but in practice, the president has the ability to dissolve the National Assembly. Moreover, President Keïta's son is the chair of the defense committee of the National Assembly. Thus, substantive roles in determining defense policy are largely restricted to the executive branch.

Ministry of Defense

Civilian oversight does exist at the Ministry of Defense, in the form of the defense minister, though most other positions appear to be held by

---

[85] Interviews with senior Gendarmerie nationale CT officers, Bamako, Mali, January 23, 2015; interview with Malian general officer, Bamako, Mali, January 22, 2015.

[86] Interview with Malian general officer, Bamako, Mali, January 22, 2015.

military. The power within the ministry still resides with the chief of the general staff. There is an audit and oversight process in place, but the ministerial inspector general (which is most likely to audit a given transaction) is not an independent body. Only the senior-most oversight body, the Vérificateur général (Auditor General), is truly independent, as evidenced by the release in 2014 of a searing audit report of military procurement.[87]

Defense Budgeting Process

Defense budgets are prepared according to the same formal process used by other ministries: The ministry drafts a budget that is reviewed by the Ministry of Economy and Finance, which conducts technical discussions on budget line items. At present, the Malian government does not utilize priority-based budgeting; however, a law will go into effect in 2016 that adopts this practice. The draft budget then heads to the National Assembly, where the Finance Committee, which can request additional discussions, reviews it. While in theory it is possible for the legislature to challenge the budget as prepared, in practice this does not happen. Once the finance law is passed, the budget must be spent, a project that requires the utilization of both *ordonnateurs* (authorizers) and *comptables* (accountants). According to a 1996 law that set forth these procedures, accountants work for the Ministry of Economy and Finance, and authorizers are ministers, whose status as authorizers is delegated through a chain of command in the ministry.[88] The Ministry of Defense has slightly different rules from the rest of government in that the accountants for the Ministry of Defense report to the defense minister, not the minister of economy and finance.[89] Despite the existence of multiple layers of the inspector general, corruption still exists at multiple levels within the defense establishment, a

---

[87] Bureau du vérificateur général, *Acquisition d'un aéronef et fourniture aux Forces armées maliennes de matériels d'habillement, de couchage, de campement, et d'alimentation (HCCA), ainsi que de véhicules et de pièces de rechange*, Bamako, Mali, October 2014.

[88] Wuyi Omitoogun and Eboe Hutchful, *Budgeting for the Military Sector in Africa: The Processes and Mechanisms of Control*, Solna and Oxford: Stockholm International Peace Research Institute and Oxford University Press, 2006, p. 129.

[89] Omitoogun and Hutchful, 2006.

point that was highlighted by several civil society watchers of the military with whom the researchers spoke.[90]

Conclusion

The FAMa do not lack plans for self-improvement. Working with the international community, the government has initiated reform processes in the areas of security sector organization, defense force structure, and doctrine. However, Mali's forces appear to have difficulty taking the next step to implement planned reforms. Moreover, while, at senior levels, some members of the FAMa and government are well aware that successful resolution of the situation in the North requires fielding armed forces with the trust of the local population, the Malian military appears unable to act in a way that inspires confidence in the military and government, and it has not made doing so a priority.[91]

These failures speak to problems of institutional culture and human capital. One senior military official repeatedly stressed the need to develop cultures around key institutional processes, such as maintenance, management, and doctrine.[92] Members of civil society described the failures as deficiencies of management, which lead to problems, such as corruption and impunity, which run throughout the government and result in an inability on the part of the FAMa to exert mechanisms of control.[93] Among the international military community in Mali, the diagnosis is similar: Often, soldiers do not obey officers' orders, and there is a poor understanding of how to treat people,

---

[90] Interviews with National Coalition of Civil Society for Peace and the Fight Against the Proliferation of Small Arms (CONASCIPAL) and National Human Rights Council personnel, Bamako, Mali, January 25, 2015.

[91] Pezard and Shurkin, 2015, pp. 40–41.

[92] Interview with Malian general officer, Bamako, Mali, January 22, 2015.

[93] Interviews with CONASCIPAL personnel, Bamako, Mali, January 25, 2015, and National Human Rights Council personnel, Bamako, Mali, January 23, 2015.

both within and outside the army.[94] Moreover, leadership within the FAMa was described as so centralized and stovepiped that leaders had to ask international actors for information on activities in other parts of the FAMa, potentially seriously hampering effectiveness.[95] These failures of command were partially responsible for the army's defeat at Kidal in early 2014, according to one senior French official.[96] It should be said that the FAMa possess numerous dedicated officers. The failures here refer to problems of command culture, education and training for leaders, and a more general need to build institutional identity and discipline throughout the ranks. There is a broad need for Mali's security forces to become "republican" with respect to their adherence to the law and the promotion of ethnic integration and cohesion.[97] This means that the soldier works for the government and, more abstractly, the nation and is responsible for the protection and trust of the people. Inadequate institutional culture and lack of leadership skills are prominent themes that run through the description of Mali's capabilities and limitations and should be understood as an essential part of developing any lasting solutions for the FAMa.

---

[94] Interview with Western European MINUSMA member, Bamako, Mali, January 26, 2015.

[95] Interview with EUTM ATF member, Bamako, Mali, January 30, 2015.

[96] Interview with French general officer, Paris, France, February 4, 2015.

[97] Interview with Malian general officer, Bamako, Mali, January 22, 2015.

CHAPTER FIVE

Malian Partners' Strategies, Capabilities, and Limitations

This chapter examines the important contributions that France, the UN, and the EU are making to building the capacity of Mali's security forces. Although all three make valuable efforts that result in clear operational and institutional improvements, they are still a long way from getting the FAMa to reach the level where it can effectively, and independently, conduct CT operations. Regardless, it is essential that the United States act in coordination with these other assistance providers.

France

France's military intervention that began in January 2013 marked a key turning point in French defense policy, with important ramifications for Mali and the region. The intervention signals, among other things, that Paris regards what it commonly refers to as the *bande saharo-sahelienne* (BSS, Sahara-Sahel band) as a front line in the defense of French and European interests and security. President François Hollande, in July 2014, during a visit to the French Air Force drone base in Niamey, said that by "assuring the security of Niger, you are assuring the security of France."[1] Paris, therefore, is committed to doing what it can within its limited resources to at least hold the

---

[1] François Hollande, "Allocution à la base aérienne de Niamey au Niger," Présidence de la République française, July 19, 2014.

line against Islamist militants and the political instability that benefits them.

French Strategy and Capabilities

Unlike Serval, which can be thought of as nothing more than an emergency response to a localized crisis in Mali, Operation Barkhane aims to cover the entire BSS. Its area of operations is the gigantic swathe of territory from the Atlantic coast of Mauritania to Chad's border with Sudan. Reflecting the strategic shift described above, Barkhane superseded not just Serval but also long-standing operations in Chad and Côte d'Ivoire (Épervier and Licorne, respectively), as well as reorients the entire French military establishment in West Africa for the purpose of fighting terrorism. Barkhane's primary targets initially were the terrorist groups active in Mauritania, Mali, and Niger and the networks that span the region and stretch into Algeria and Libya. Recently, however, France has included under Barkhane's mandate its growing involvement in the conflict against Boko Haram, which has been spilling across borders in the Lake Chad region and has drawn in the staunch French allies Chad and Cameroon. Paris in early March 2015 announced that it would reinforce Barkhane—which initially had about 3,000 soldiers—with additional troops specifically for the purpose of countering Boko Haram in what might be thought of as the Lake Chad theater.[2]

Barkhane, as of September 2015, boasts 3,500 troops and has at its disposal 17 helicopters of various types, 200 armored vehicles, 200 logistics vehicles, six to ten fixed-wing transport aircraft, eight fighter planes, and five drones.[3] These are divided among several locations, including Atar, Mauritania; Gao and Tessalit, Mali; Niamey, Niger; and Abéché, Faya-Largeau, and N'Djaména, Chad (see Figure 5.1). The two major bases are in Gao and N'Djaména. Elements and facili-

---

[2]   Laurent Lagneau, "Sahel: Les effectifs de l'opération Barkhane vont augmenter; Deux militaires français gravement blessés au Mali," *Zone Militaire*, March 11, 2015.

[3]   French Ministry of Defense, "Carte Operation Barkhane," Paris, updated December 3, 2015; email from French officer in the French Army General Staff, August 3, 2015.

Figure 5.1
Map of Operation Barkhane

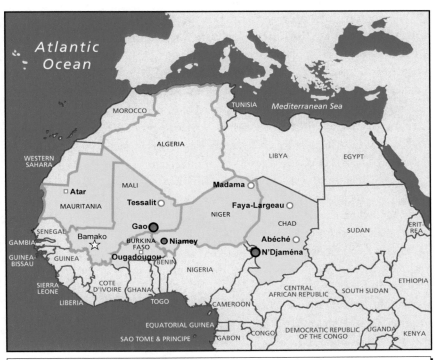

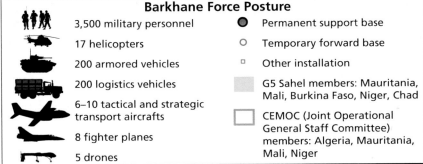

SOURCE: French Ministry of Defense, 2015.
RAND RR1241-5.1

ties in Senegal, Côte d'Ivoire, Cameroon, and Gabon assist with logistical support and provide a reserve capability.

Geography arguably constitutes a major challenge to French operations: More than 2,000 miles separate Atar from Faya-Largeau; Tessalit is 800 miles from Bamako and roughly 300 miles from Gao. For all intents and purposes, there are no paved roads in most of the region. Thus, everything must be transported by air using France's limited lift capacity or over what often amounts to no more than dirt tracks. The other major challenge is the small size of the French force. Thirty-five hundred soldiers in so large an area of operations is a very small number. Of course, the French during Serval demonstrated their ability to operate effectively in the BSS and accomplish a lot with very little. They have a force structure geared for light and mobile operations, including light wheeled armored vehicles well suited for the terrain (and relatively easy to transport by air) and an operating style that enables them rapidly to pull together and field autonomous company-scale combined arms task forces and reform them on the fly, as needs dictate.[4] This is useful when one needs to spread one's forces thin, conduct multiple small-scale operations simultaneously, and move around quickly with limited transportation and logistical resources. Moreover, the French have more than a century of experience operating in the BSS and know the human terrain exceptionally well. They know how to interoperate effectively with host-nation security forces and use them to supplement their own numbers. For example, during the first week of March 2015, 40 French troops from Barkhane "deployed in support" of a mission in which roughly 700 Mauritanian and 500 Malian soldiers conducted a reconnaissance mission in the Forest of Ouagadou, which reportedly has become a bastion of Islamist activity.[5]

The fact remains, though, that as good as the French are at making the most of limited resources, there is only so much one can do in so great a geographic area against diffuse opponents. For example, according to one press report, "tactical mobility is constrained by

---

[4]   On these issues, see Michael Shurkin, *France's War in Mali: Lessons for an Expeditionary Army*, Santa Monica, Calif.: RAND Corporation, RR-770-A, 2014.

[5]   "Barkhane: Point du situation du 12 mars," French Ministry of Defense, March 12, 2015.

the insufficient number of helicopters, and politico-military ambitions run up against capability limits."[6] France not only has too few helicopters but also has no heavy-lift helicopters, such as CH-47s, in its inventory. There is also the question of France's focus on going after high-value targets, which perhaps reflects the limitations of France's resources. A leading French military analyst and commentator, Colonel Michel Goya, questioned the value over the long term of leading such a "minimal mission" when so much more would be required to "win" in the BSS:

> If a good strategy must accord ends with means, the volume and the form of the military deployment put in place does not leave any alternative other than trying to contain the [armed terrorist groups] outside of the states of the Sahel. However, aside from the fact that a strategy of targeted elimination will end up being questioned in France, as has been the case elsewhere, this minimal mission will be difficult to conduct over the long term. The enemy groups dispose of rear bases in countries (Algeria, Libya) where there is no, for the moment, question of intervening, and one cannot envision in the near term their being destroyed by local forces. Above all, the French deployment is taking place in a region in which the factors of instability—ethnic, demographic, ecological, economic—are deep, durable, and affect everyone involved in the conflict, as with the endemic conflict between the Malian state and the Tuaregs. To be coherent, French strategy must associate the actions of all the ministries in a common vision. Does this common vision exist among the different ministries? This, too, is not clear.[7]

Goya concluded his post by asking whether France, now that it finds itself on the front line in Africa, will "truly assume this burden" and give itself the means to succeed—presumably by investing in its mili-

---

[6] Frédéric Lert, "Sahel: La guerre aride," *Science et Vie*, special issue, *Spécial Aviation*, 2015, p. 45.

[7] Michel Goya, "La voie de l'épée: Extension du domaine de la lutte," *La Voie de l'Épée*, May 2014; our translation.

tary and other capabilities so as to significantly boost the scale of its effort.

Now, more than a year after Goya's analysis, it seems that, for a variety of policy reasons, Paris is making the best of the means at Barkhane's disposal with the objective of holding the line. When asked about French ambitions in the BSS, French officials we interviewed in Paris stressed their confidence that Barkhane was making a valuable contribution to French security and, at the very least, was better than doing nothing.[8] Budgetary constraints and other strategic priorities—such as Operation Sentinelle, the reinforced surveillance of the French territory following the Paris attacks of January 2015—make it unlikely that France can spare more forces to Mali, or even sustain Barkhane at the current level in the long term. Sentinelle effectively ties down nearly half of the troops available to France at any time, given its force-generation cycle, and is placing such a strain on the French military that it might have to alter that cycle, with cascading effects on readiness and French operations elsewhere, including in the BSS.

These limits mean that if the United States wishes to see greater French success in the BSS, it will have to contribute more to the French effort. U.S. boots on the ground under French command probably would make a significant difference, although that scenario is implausible. This would be an ideal opportunity for a RAF, given the value of learning how to interoperate with the French in West Africa and ideally learn from them. U.S. SOF likely would strengthen French operations. Supplying more-strategic lift would alleviate some of the financial burden of Barkhane on the French, who, absent their own strategic lift, are leasing it from private contractors. Intratheater lift and helicopters would enhance France's tactical mobility and thus enable it to do more with the troops it has.

---

[8] Interview with French officials, Paris, France, February 4, 2015; interview with French general officer, Paris, France, February 4, 2015.

The United Nations Multidimensional Integrated Stabilization Mission in Mali

While Serval was concluding what might be described as the "major combat operations" phase of its mission, the UN Security Council, on April 25, 2013, established MINUSMA, which superseded the earlier African-Led International Support Mission in Mali and had as its primary mission stabilizing the country in the wake of the crisis, while the French focused on targeting the jihadi groups.[9]

Often labeled the world's deadliest peacekeeping mission because of the high number of attacks against its personnel,[10] the UN mission in Mali consists of roughly 11,500 personnel, though its uniformed component is roughly 1,000 fewer than authorized.[11] These uniformed personnel consist of

- 9,142 military personnel
- 1,178 police (including formed units)
- 523 international civilian personnel
- 542 local civilian staff
- 125 UN volunteers.[12]

The mission has military contributions from 41 nations and police contributions from 29.

The MINUSMA force structure is generally focused on a northern presence, with brigade-level headquarters located in Gao, Kidal, and Timbuktu and a division-level headquarters in Bamako. The primary maneuver forces for the mission come from Burkina Faso, Senegal, and Bangladesh, and there is a SOF contingent from Chad. In Gao, there is a Dutch SOF element equipped with Apache attack helicopters, which

---

[9]   United Nations Security Council, Resolution 2100, April 25, 2013.

[10]   See, for instance, CIVIC, 2015, p. 5.

[11]   "MINUSMA Facts and Figures," United Nations Multidimensional Integrated Stabilization Mission in Mali, June 25, 2014.

[12]   "MINUSMA Facts and Figures," United Nations Multidimensional Integrated Stabilization Mission in Mali, May 19, 2015.

is mirrored by the Swedes (minus the Apaches) in Timbuktu.[13] Both are conducting long-range reconnaissance and intelligence, surveillance, and reconnaissance (ISR) missions, according to a Western European MINUSMA officer.[14] The MINUSMA effort also features a first-of-its-kind intelligence-like cell, the All Sources Information Fusion Unit (ASIFU).[15] This unit is composed of intelligence officers from a variety of northern European militaries (Danish, Dutch, Finn, German, Norwegian, Swedish, etc.) who, using an information technology infrastructure provided by the Dutch military intelligence service, work to assemble a complete situational-awareness picture, going beyond studying the armed groups to analyzing political, military, economic, social, and infrastructure aspects of the situation.[16] The unit gathers information by means of Scan Eagle and Raven unmanned aerial vehicles, as well as by field surveys conducted by Dutch SOF in Gao.[17] Because of the large number of nations in the larger MINUSMA contingent, some of which ASIFU participants would prefer not to share information with, ASIFU, with the UN's permission, shares information with MINUSMA on a selective basis.

MINUSMA Strategy and Capabilities

The Mali mission is, for the UN, part of a newer kind of mission, called a *stabilization mission* or *robust peacekeeping*. While *stabilization* is not a well-defined term for the UN, robust peacekeeping is the "use of force by the [UN contributor-nation] military in situations that are not wars."[18] In this case, the lack of a peace agreement until recently complicated the peacekeeping mission, because there was technically no peace to enforce; instead, the UN's initial mandate in Mali was to

---

[13] Interview with MINUSMA official, Bamako, Mali, January 26, 2015.

[14] Interview with Western European MINUSMA officer, Bamako, Mali, January 26, 2015.

[15] "Peacekeeping Operations," Norway Mission to the United Nations, December 17, 2014.

[16] Ministerie van of Defensie (Netherlands), *NL bijdrage uitgelicht: Factsheet inlichtingen (ASIFU) MINUSMA*, The Hague, May 2014, p. 3.

[17] Ministerie van of Defensie (Netherlands), 2014, p. 3.

[18] Thierry Tardy, "A Critique of Robust Peacekeeping in Contemporary Peace Operations," *International Peacekeeping*, Vol. 18, No. 2, April 2011, p. 153.

provide the "stabilization of key population centers and support for the reestablishment of State authority throughout the country," as well as to support the transitional authority road map.[19] In June 2014, the UN augmented the mandate to underscore the security aspect of the mission ("to deter threats and take active steps to prevent the return of armed elements to those areas"), to enhance operational coordination with the Malian uniformed services, and to support the peace process.[20] Then and now, even after the signing of the Algiers Accords, MINUSMA has had to walk a fine line between actively supporting the Malian state and its efforts to extend its authority and not becoming a full-fledged military ally. For example, according to a Western European officer in MINUSMA, MINUSMA can coordinate operations with the FAMa but not conduct joint operations; the difference, however, often boils down to semantics that might be lost on locals.[21] The CAGs have been quick to accuse MINUSMA of partisanship and likely will continue to do so as Bamako and the northern rebel groups inch toward establishing the new modus vivendi outlined roughly by the Algiers Accords. The most notorious example of alleged collusion is MINUSMA's intervention in a clash in Tabankort in January, when Dutch Apaches fired on MNLA fighters who were clashing with GATIA (the Dutch said that the MNLA was firing rockets at MINUSMA positions, so they acted to take out the rocket launcher).[22] Nonetheless, MINUSMA appears to provide a benefit to civilians in northern Mali. While some argued that MINUSMA locations drew fire, endangering those who gathered near them for safety, others indicated that they put pressure on violent groups and at the very least keep the situation from getting significantly worse.[23]

---

[19] United Nations Security Council, 2013, p. 7.

[20] United Nations Security Council, 2014a, p. 6.

[21] Interview with Western European MINUSMA officer, Bamako, Mali, January 26, 2015.

[22] "UN Holds Talks to Calm North Mali Town as Armed Groups Clash," 2015; David Lewis and Emma Farge, "Dutch UN Attack Helicopters Strike Mali Rebels in North," Reuters, January 20, 2015.

[23] Interview with U.S. MINUSMA officers, Bamako, Mali, January 25, 2015.

Perhaps MINUSMA's central difficulty is the tension between its political requirements and its military realities. For example, while the revised mandate directs the organization to "expand its presence, including through long-range patrols and within its capacities, in the North of Mali beyond key population centers, notably in areas where civilians are at risk," militarily the organization is struggling to maintain supply routes to existing locations.[24] If this were primarily a military mission, the force would extend north as its support capabilities warranted; however, with a mandate to protect civilians, it must be present in those areas where civilians are endangered. This creates inefficiencies and vulnerabilities for MINUSMA, as a great deal of effort is expended on securing supply convoys, and forces are pushed into static positions as a result of military necessity. As one respondent put it, the "only ops are for survival," rather than security or civil-military relations.[25] This situation may improve as the MINUSMA laydown is filled out over the rest of the mandate period.

A final challenge for MINUSMA is the capabilities of the contributing nations shouldering the load in the North—specifically, Burkina Faso, Senegal, Bangladesh, and Chad. For example, with the escalation of insecurity in northern Mali and the rise in the use of IEDs and land mines, these forces are especially vulnerable, as they lack proper training and equipment to handle these threats.[26] These forces also appear to lack adequate equipment for effectively countering or offering protection from IEDs. Similarly, many MINUSMA contingents reportedly struggle with static defense (securing facilities). Some are said to do a poor job at intelligence.[27] To be fair, MINUSMA duty might not play to different contingents' strengths: Chadians, for instance, are notoriously good at offensive operations, qualities that do not apply readily to peacekeeping duties.

---

[24] United Nations Security Council, 2014b, p. 6; interview with U.S. MINUSMA officials, Bamako, Mali, January 25, 2015.

[25] Interview with U.S. MINUSMA officials, Bamako, Mali, January 25, 2015.

[26] Interview with Western European MINUSMA officers, Bamako, Mali, January 26, 2015; interview with U.S. MINUSMA officers, Bamako, Mali, January 25, 2015.

[27] Interview with Western European MINUSMA officer, Bamako, Mali, January 26, 2015.

The European Union Training Mission

EUTM is an EU-backed multinational training mission consisting of roughly 500 soldiers from more than a dozen EU member-states based in Bamako and Koulikoro, where it conducts most of its work. EUTM predates Serval in that it was planned in 2012, but the events of January 2013 accelerated its deployment. Its first mandate began in February of that year; in May 2014, its mandate was extended until 2016. EUTM represents both France's need to improve Malian Army capabilities—with the hope that France might be able to reduce its activities in the region as Mali becomes increasingly able to provide security itself—and desire to spread the burden by, in effect, delegating the project to the EU and asking EU states to provide at least some of the required personnel, money, and material. EUTM draws from many nations and currently is under the command of a Spanish general; however, France has consistently provided the largest single contingent and, until recently, EUTM's commanders.

EUTM's objectives at least initially were relatively ambitious. Not only did it aspire to elevate the Malian Army's operational effectiveness and readiness but it also aimed to reform the army, schooling it in values that Western militaries associate with professionalism and making it into something comparable to the republican army described earlier. Thus, EUTM's first commander, the French General François Lecointre, told *Jeune Afrique*:

> We have the rather ambitious objective of regenerating, refounding, and reconstructing the Malian Army so that it is at once operationally effective and respectful of the rule of law. To that end, our mission rests on two pillars: on one hand, a mission consisting of auditing and providing expertise and counsel to Malian military authorities; on the other, a training mission. This army has to become one of the pillars of the modern Malian state.[28]

---

[28] Benjamin Roger, "Général Lecointre: 'Il faut que l'armée devienne l'un des piliers de l'État malien,'" *Jeune Afrique*, March 18, 2013; our translation.

It follows that EUTM ostensibly includes in its curriculum training in such matters as the law of war and human rights law, and because of its practice of training ethnically mixed classes whose members are drawn from an array of regiments, the EUTM experience potentially contributes to the kind of ethnic and unit integration that the army desperately needs. Speaking at an event in Brussels, Lecointre spoke of the FAMa's need to serve as a "crucible of the nation."[29] He explained that although he "did not enter into ethnic considerations," the fact is that they "pose themselves." For example, EUTM uses French even though many of the soldiers do not speak it, making the language potentially a unifying factor since the language is not associated with any ethnic group in particular and also provides a common tongue as non–French speakers get up to speed. Similarly, he said, there were between 130 and 150 Tuaregs in the first battalion formed by EUTM, and the French made sure that there were relatively evenly distributed throughout to ensure that they were not isolated and did not isolate themselves.[30]

The major effort of EUTM's training mission in Mali has been to develop a new structure based on the GTIA. A GTIA is an operational construct based on a French model that builds on an infantry backbone, adding specialized skills, such as artillery, infantry, reconnaissance, cavalry, or sappers, as needed, similar to an operational task force. EUTM pulls from existing army regiments' battalion-sized task forces, each with 610 soldiers.[31] They include a "commando detachment" of 36 men, an armored squadron with about 50 soldiers and a dozen BTR-60s, three infantry companies (140 men), a support platoon with recoilless rifles and 60-mm mortars, an engineering company, an artillery battery (with GRAD-2M rocket launchers), and a support and logistics company.[32]

---

[29] Thomas Le Bihan, "Réussites et manques: Bilan des six premiers mois d'EUTM Mali (Lecointre)," *Bruxelles2*, July 21, 2013.

[30] Le Bihan, 2013.

[31] "Mission Update Briefing," European Union Training Mission in Mali, November 17, 2014.

[32] Touchard, 2014c.

EUTM gives the soldiers new uniforms and equipment and submits them to a 12-week training regimen.[33] They receive group training primarily in basic infantry tactics and some in other areas, including human rights.[34] Next the components of the GTIAs receive additional specialized skill training for their type. Finally, the units are rotated through active service in the North. While the GTIAs generally appear to have improved on the raw skills of the soldiers, the level of training appears to be more that of basic infantry tactics than of collective training, which enables combined arms operations.

To date, EUTM has trained six GTIAs and aims to train a total of eight before the end of the current mandate, while periodically putting the older GTIAs through seven-week refresher courses. EUTM also conducts an 11-week company commander's course for GTIA commanders, a 14-week train-the-trainer course, and a 13-week "combat river crossing training course."[35] The GTIAs now represent the pointy end of the FAMa's spear, the maneuver units tasked with rotations in the North. EUTM also operates the ATF, consisting of 18 officers placed throughout the army to "support the reform process" and provide "audit and technical advisory support."[36] The ATF's purpose is to advise the army and support the general reform process.

It is difficult to evaluate EUTM's success. EUTM officers interviewed for this study said that they had no metrics beyond the numbers of soldiers who have been through the process and the numbers of GTIAs produced.[37] The catastrophic Kidal offensive of May 2014, which involved the EUTM-trained GTIA 4 Balanzan, underscores just how far the FAMa have to go. While the training is helpful, it focuses on basic skills and reportedly does not aim to prepare Malians for battalion-level operations. For example, a Western European officer with MINUSMA explained that the FAMa contingent in Timbuktu

---

[33] "Mission Update Briefing," 2014.

[34] "GTIA 'Al Farouk,'" European Union Training Mission in Mali, January 28, 2015.

[35] "Mission Update Briefing," 2014.

[36] "Mission Update Briefing," 2014.

[37] Interview with EUTM officers, Bamako, Mali, January 30, 2015.

was largely static; however, he speculated that the possible arrival of an EUTM-trained GTIA might bring about a shift toward greater activity.[38] That said, he observed, "EUTM does not train for operations, just basic infantry skills."

The leaders responsible for the May 2014 Kidal attack did not appreciate this distinction when they ordered the battalion-sized attack.[39] The operation revealed that, in fact, EUTM GTIAs cannot conduct coordinated operations. Moreover, the debacle revealed other failures having to do with basics, such as sustaining troops in the field.[40] The EUTM officers we interviewed seven months later were quick to distance themselves from the failure and reject the implication that it put their efforts in a bad light.[41] Among other things, they pointed to the fact that they do not train GTIAs to conduct coordinated operations. (They also noted that whoever organized the Kidal attack created a hybrid force with elements from GTIAs and troops from other units, which made coordination all the more difficult and demonstrated poor planning.) Given the value of EUTM's contributions, which no one contests, Kidal makes clear that EUTM simply is not sufficient if the goal is getting Mali's army to the point where it can conduct the mission identified by U.S. SOF prior to 2012 of being able to mount a complex attack against a fixed position at a great distance. EUTM also is not covering the kind of long-endurance patrolling in the context of the Garde nationale's camel corps. And EUTM officers made clear that they do not invest much energy into training that would boost the army's republican qualities: "We don't do it because it's not our priority."[42]

It also is not clear how personnel assignments to the GTIAs function, as well as whether this promotes or erodes larger institutional

---

[38] Interview with Western European MINUSMA officer, Bamako, Mali, January 26, 2015.

[39] Touchard, 2014b.

[40] "Véritable carnage à Kidal: Enième humiliation ou débout de la reconquête armée?" *Malijet*, May 20, 2014.

[41] Interview with EUTM officers, Bamako, Mali, January 30, 2015.

[42] Interview with EUTM officers, Bamako, Mali, January 30, 2015.

capacity. For example, if a GTIA returns from rotation and the soldiers return to their garrison units, will the same soldiers rejoin the GTIA when it re-forms? Meanwhile, what sort of training is provided to the rest of Mali's security services, the rest of the time?

The bottom line for EUTM appears to be that, while it is helping, it cannot be expected to accomplish much given the relatively short training period allocated to each GTIA; the GTIA-by-GTIA approach, which is not the same as a comprehensive training program; and issues related to the ephemeral nature of GTIAs and the skills provided to soldiers once they return to their home units. It is not, moreover, a substitute for a FAMa-wide training program and reforming how the FAMa recruit soldiers and what the FAMa do with those recruits from initial boot camp to unit formation and beyond. Moreover, despite EUTM's stated interest in providing training in such matters as humanitarian law and ethnic issues, it is clear that it does not make them the priorities they should be, in part because of the limited time and resources with which EUTM works. It does not make "conduct" a training priority; EUTM officers noted that some Malians resist integrating their forces but do not make a point of integration.[43] Given the FAMa's fundamental inability to operate in the North without antagonizing local communities, EUTM's focus on basic operational skills, though understandable, might be insufficient.

However, an awareness of the shortfalls in EUTM's activities should help guide any future U.S. training efforts. For example, if EUTM is not sufficiently pushing republican values, the United States could. If EUTM is not moving on to more-advanced coordinated maneuvers, or if it is not helping Mali's army develop the kind of long-endurance patrolling that it requires, U.S. trainers could focus on those issues. Given that EUTM appears to be an enduring mission, EUTM might also be an appropriate target for outreach by AFRICOM's RAF troops, which most likely would benefit from interacting with EUTM—by learning from its experience and obtaining a better understanding of the security assistance mission in West Africa in general—while offering EUTM additional resources in return.

---

[43] Interviews with EUTM officers, Bamako, Mali, January 30, 2015.

The European Capacity Building Mission Mali

EUCAP commenced operations in January 2015 alongside EUTM. In contrast with EUTM, which focuses on the army, EUCAP's purpose is to work with Mali's three internal security services (Gendarmerie nationale, Garde nationale, and Police nationale) to develop their capabilities. EUCAP's mission, moreover, has less of a tactical focus (although it does that, too) and more of a focus on bureaucratic and procedural matters relevant to the proper functioning of the three services as institutions.[44] EUCAP has an authorized staff of 80, and its 2015 budget was €11.4 million.[45] One of its objectives is training 600 Malian officers from different services. EUCAP provides each officer four weeks of individual training and 100 hours on such subjects as "command," judicial police, local policing, "technical and scientific policing," and human rights.[46] EUCAP is also mandated to provide specialized training in, among other subjects, CT and counter–organized crime operations, auditing services, human resources support, and logistics.

Given the crucial importance of the activities of the internal security services that EUCAP assists, however, the U.S. government should find ways to coordinate U.S. interagency programs designed to complement EUCAP efforts. As with EUTM, direct support might not make sense, but filling in gaps does. Close communication and coordination with EUCAP are essential.

Conclusion

The above survey of Mali's chief international partners in the CT fight—France, the UN, and the EU—suggest that any engagement by the United States would not be taking place in a vacuum; others are actively working to advance the same aims as the United States.

---

[44] For an overview of EUCAP, see European Union External Action, *Common Security and Defence Policy: The EUCAP Sahel Mali Civilian Mission*, Brussels, March 2015.

[45] A. Diarra, "Mali: Eucap Sahel Mali: Un soutien multiforme," *Maliactu*, 2015.

[46] Diarra, 2015.

Each partner brings certain strengths to the table and is making valuable contributions to Mali's security. Each, however, has weaknesses or limitations, such that the sufficiency of these efforts combined is doubtful, particularly in light of the upsurge in terrorist attacks. Mali undeniably is better off for these partners' efforts. However, making the region more secure will require something more.

The United States should at the very least work in close coordination with Mali's other partners and seek to achieve complementarity. The available evidence suggests that the United States and France prior to 2012 did not collaborate to the full extent that they could have in their activities on behalf of the 33e RCP and the 62e RIM. An open and continuous conversation at all levels with the French, MINUSMA, and EUTM and EUCAP should be a priority, if only to be able to understand what they are not doing and what, perhaps, the United States might do to fill in gaps.

More ambitiously, the United States might find ways to increase support to its international partners. Direct troop contributions would help significantly: This is an opportunity for AFRICOM's RAF to deploy in partnership with the French and perhaps under their command. Short of that, the United States already provides assistance to Barkhane in the form of aerial refueling, lift, and ISR; there remain opportunities to provide more. With respect to lift, for example, the French have limited intratheater lift and few helicopters, which limits their ability to shift forces around Barkhane's enormous area of operation and restricts their tactical mobility. U.S. helicopter units—above all CH-47s—would be tantamount to a force multiplier. When asked what, if anything, he would like to borrow from the U.S. inventory, a Serval commander responded, "Chinooks."[47] Even simply supplying helicopters dedicated to medical evacuation support would free up French helicopters for operational purposes, while also potentially improving the care afforded to wounded French and other soldiers.

Assisting MINUSMA directly or bilaterally with MINUSMA contributing nations also presents myriad opportunities. MINUSMA contingents lack specific skills, including countering IEDs, and often

---

[47] Interview with French officer, June 24, 2013.

leave much to be desired with respect to such tasks as static defense. There might also be ways to collaborate with the ASIFU intelligence fusion cell, particularly given its arm's length relationship with the rest of MINUSMA. Predeployment training has also been cited as a way the United States could contribute to MINUSMA.

With respect to EUTM and EUCAP, there is a clear need to coordinate whatever training the United States might provide with EUTM and EUCAP to ensure complementarity or at least to avoid problems associated with teaching Malians techniques different from those taught by the Europeans. Presumably by communicating with EUTM and EUCAP, the U.S. country team should be able to identify weaknesses or shortfalls in the training provided by the Europeans that the United States might help to address.

CHAPTER SIX

Conclusion

Mali cannot handle the terrorist threat in its territory without outside help. The task before the United States is to identify opportunities to engage with Mali and its other international partners to bring greater security and stability to Mali and the region. Given the nature of recurrent conflicts in northern Mali, peace and prosperity appear distant prospects at best. That said, there are ways to at least increase Mali's capabilities while at the same time making Bamako a better steward of its northern population, and making the FAMa a net contributor to security rather than a contributor to insecurity.

A number of Malian leaders recognize the need to adopt a more global approach that includes humanitarian efforts and various forms of civic engagement intended to foster better relations between the FAMa and Mali's northern populations and, consequently, boost Bamako's legitimacy. That said, they appear to prioritize quickly acquiring tactical capabilities that would enable them to perform better on the battlefield.

Among the problems with Mali's interest in acquiring offensive military capabilities is the strong likelihood that the FAMa will succeed only in exacerbating preexisting tensions in the North. Given the failure of those security assistance efforts and the need to elevate the quality of all of the FAMa by assisting with basic, fundamental capabilities and processes, the solution might be to help Mali acquire the offensive capability it wants while prioritizing the force's professional or republican qualities as much as its tactical ones. If one focuses only on providing Malian units with warfighting skills, the units might do well in battle but can be counted on to antagonize locals. The FAMa might win battles but lose the war. A more republican FAMa, a force that does not treat northerners like foreigners and is not in turn perceived as alien by northerners, will have a better chance of winning the war—i.e., bringing security to Mali. That force will also likely be more effective on the battlefield given better unit cohesion and the improved integration of northerners who will be less likely to desert and be better situated to provide the FAMa with expertise and local connections.

Otherwise, there are few capabilities or types of equipment that the Malians do not need: The emphasis should be on capabilities suited for the FAMa's internal security mission in the North. Three particular types of operations the FAMa needs to strengthen are complex attacks on fixed positions, long-endurance patrols, and static defense. Mobility should be a priority. Conversely, it would also be valuable, given the FAMa's limited resources and poor logistical and sustainment capabilities, to encourage the FAMa as much as possible to abandon capabilities and systems that have little value and are net burdens for the FAMa (even if they would be valuable if Mali could maintain them and sustain their operations). Examples of equipment Mali needs include light all-terrain utility vehicles and basic radios, as well as uniform sets of firearms and full sets of magazines and magazine pouches. Examples of equipment that are ill suited for Mali's requirements or that Mali cannot use appropriately and thus are more of a burden than a strength include the FAMa's legacy Cold War–era Soviet-built armored vehicles. Similarly, U.S. assistance strengthening the FAMa's ability to conduct the kind of long-endurance patrols that would interact with local populations, along the lines of the old camel-mounted colonial auxiliaries—a capability currently residing in the Garde nationale—would be valuable. Such a capability requires certain equipment, including forms of communication, but mainly needs appropriate skills and procedures, ranging from recruitment practices to learning how to work with civilians.

The United States would help Mali best by discouraging hasty appropriations and using what leverage it has to encourage Mali's military and political leadership to embrace the need to carry out fundamental reforms and, benefiting from the breathing room provided by France and the UN, embrace a "slow and steady wins the race" approach to building a potent military force. Finally, the United States must try to impress on the Malians the need to focus on developing the FAMa's republican qualities, starting perhaps with the question of how to integrate rebel fighters, as required by the Algiers Accords.

The United States should strive to work cooperatively with Mali's other international partners to ensure complementarity; the "parallel play" that characterized U.S. and French efforts prior to 2012 is wasteful and possibly counterproductive. The United States should also do more to help Barkhane, which suffers from the limitations on France's resources. Ongoing support with respect to aerial refueling, lift, and ISR is valuable. It should be noted that when we asked directly what the United States can do to help, the one thing a senior French officer pointed to was the value of aerial tankers. According to him, tankers made it possible to keep French attack aircraft on station during operations, as well as to quickly direct them to attack targets or provide close support.[1] Such support should be increased whenever practical. In addition, any conventional or Special Forces ground element would help the French effort. This is an opportunity for AFRICOM to deploy forces in partnership with the French and perhaps under their command. Short of that, contributions in the form of fixed-wing or rotary-wing aircraft likely would make a significant contribution to the French effort by enhancing French tactical mobility. France has few aircraft in theater, and the French military has no heavy-lift helicopters, such as CH-47s, in its inventory. Even helping France with its medical evacuation requirements, for example, would free up scarce helicopters for combat operations.

Although this is largely self-evident, anything that the United States can do to help MINUSMA improve its capabilities or facilitate its operations is likely to be useful for countering Mali's terrorist threat and generating security for Mali's population. Two particular requirements that the United States might be able to help with are counter-IED and static defense. It might also be possible to work with MINUSMA contributing forces during predeployment training. ASIFU, because it

---

[1]   Interview with French general officer, Paris, France, February 4, 2015.

keeps its intelligence to within a "circle of friends" and exercises discretion regarding what it shares with the rest of MINUSMA, might facilitate intelligence sharing in the sense that providing information to ASIFU is not tantamount to giving it to all of MINUSMA.

EUTM and EUCAP should be regarded as an opportunity for the United States to help the Malians substantively, though indirectly, given that these two programs are forging a deep and enduring relationship with the FAMa. Maintaining an open dialogue with EUTM and EUCAP should be a priority, and the aim of that dialogue should be to identify ways to second EUTM's and EUCAP's efforts either directly or indirectly, by pursuing independent but complementary and coordinated training efforts.

The stakes, at this point, are clearer than ever. The January 2013 offensive by Islamists that threatened Bamako itself indicates that the Islamist groups in Mali threaten the country's viability and pose a danger to the entire region and beyond: There is the threat represented by the use of northern Mali as a base for wide-ranging operations, potentially against Europe and the United States. There is also the threat represented by the potential destruction of the Malian state, which is certain to have significant negative ramifications for all of Mali's neighbors, each of which already has its own problems with radicalization and insecurity. As hard as "fixing" or at least stabilizing Mali will be, generating security in the region will be all the more difficult the further the situation in Mali degrades.

Finally, given the complexity of the situation in northern Mali, peace and prosperity appear to be distant prospects. U.S. policymakers should take to heart the presence of real talent among Mali's military leadership, as well as the commitment of Mali's international partners to improving the country's security and stability and strengthening Mali's prospects. One must not overlook the fact that all the available evidence suggests that militancy—jihadi or not—has a highly limited appeal among Malians, and the "troublemakers" historically have never represented more than just a small fraction of northern Malian society. The vast majority of Malians, northern and southern, wants—needs—Mali as a country to succeed.

Abbreviations

AFP	Agence France-Presse
AFRICOM	U.S. Africa Command
AQIM	al-Qaeda in the Islamic Maghreb
ASIFU	All Sources Information Fusion Unit (MINUSMA)
ATF	Advisory Task Force (EUTM)
ATNM	Alliance-Touareg-Niger-Mali (Niger-Mali-Tuareg Alliance)
ATT	Amadou Toumani Touré (president of Mali)
BSS	bande Saharo-Sahelienne (Sahara-Sahel band)
CAG	Compliant Armed Group
CEMOC	Comité d'état-major opérationnel conjoint (Regional Command for Joint Counterterrorism Operations)
CFS	Compagnie forces spéciales (Special Forces Company)
CIVIC	Civilians in Conflict
CMA	Coordination des mouvements de l'Azawad (Coordination of Azawad Movements)

CMFPR	Coordination des mouvements et fronts patriotiques de résistance (Coordination of Movements and Fronts of Patriotic Resistance)
COIN	counterinsurgency
CPA	Coalition du peuple de l'Azawad (Azawad People Coalition)
CT	counterterrorism
DDR	disarmament, demobilization, and reintegration
DGSE	Direction générale de la sécurité extérieure (Directorate-General for External Security)
DSART	Defense Sector Assessment Rating Tool
EOD	explosive ordnance disposal
ETIA	Echelon tactique interarme (Combined Arms Tactical Echelon)
EU	European Union
EUCAP	European Union Capacity Building Mission
EUTM	European Union Training Mission in Mali
FAMa	Forces armées maliennes (Malian armed forces)
FM	field manual
GATIA	Groupe autodéfense touareg Imghad et alliés (Imghad Tuareg and Allies Self-Defense Group)
GSPC	Groupe Salafiste de la prédication et le combat (Salafist Preaching and Combat Group)
GTIA	groupement tactique interarme

HCUA	Haut conseil pour l'unité de l'Azawad (High Council for the Unity of Azawad)
HUMINT	human intelligence
ICRC	International Committee of the Red Cross
IED	improvised explosive device
ISR	intelligence, surveillance, and reconnaissance
JCET	Joint Combined Exchange Training
JPAT	Joint Planning and Assistance Team
JSOTF-TS	Joint Special Operations Task Force–Trans Sahara
LOPM	Loi d'orientation et de programmation militaire (Military Orientation and Planning Law)
MAA	Mouvement arabe de l'Azawad (Arab Movement of Azawad)
MINUSMA	United Nations Multidimensional Integrated Stabilization Mission in Mali
MNLA	Mouvement national de libération de l'Azawad (National Movement for the Liberation of Azawad)
MUJAO	Mouvement pour l'unicité et le jihad en Afrique de l'ouest (Movement for Oneness and Jihad in West Africa)
PIGN	Peloton d'intervention de la Gendarmerie nationale (National Gendarmerie Intervention Platoon)
PSI	Pan-Sahel Initiative
PSPDN	Programme pour la paix, la sécurité, et le développement au Nord-Mali (Program for Peace, Security, and Development in Northern Mali)
RAF	Regionally Aligned Forces

RCP	Régiment de commandos parachutistes (Paratroopers Commando Regiment)
RIM	Régiment d'infanterie motorisé (Motorized Infantry Regiment)
SIGINT	signals intelligence
SIRH	Système d'information des ressources humaines (Human Resources Information System)
SOF	special operations forces
TSCTP	Trans-Saharan Counterterrorism Partnership
UN	United Nations
UNMAS	United Nations Mine Action Service
USAID	U.S. Agency for International Development

References

11th Parachute Brigade, briefing, Fort Bragg, N.C., June 23, 2013.

"About UNMAS in Mali," United Nations Mine Action Service, December 2014.

AFP—*See* Agence France-Presse.

Agence France-Presse, "Suspected Al-Qaeda Members Kill Malian Army Officer," June 11, 2009.

———, "Mali: Nouvelle attaque d'une localité dans le centre, un civil tué," *Africa No. 1*, January 7, 2015a. As of May 19, 2015:
http://www.africa1.com/spip.php?article51337

———, "Suspect in Bamako Restaurant Bombing Killed, Mali Says," *France 24*, March 13, 2015b. As of May 19, 2015:
http://www.france24.com/en/
20150313-suspect-bamako-restaurant-bombing-killed-mali/

———, "Après la mort d'un de ses employés, le CICR suspend ses déplacements dans le nord du Mali," aBamako.com, April 1, 2015c. As of May 23, 2015:
http://news.abamako.com/h/83244.html

———, "Nord du Mali: Attentat suicide contre une base de l'ONU, 3 morts," *Le Nouvel Observateur*, April 15, 2015d. As of May 19, 2015:
http://tempsreel.nouvelobs.com/topnews/20150415.AFP4958/mali-attentat-suicide-contre-une-base-des-casques-bleus-3-morts.html

Ahmed, Baba, "Mali: Deux ans après Serval, AQMI reprend ses quartiers au Nord de Tombouctou," *Jeune Afrique*, January 9, 2015.

"Al-Qaeda in the Islamic Maghreb," *Jane's World Insurgency and Terrorism*, October 22, 2014.

"Al-Qaeda-Linked Group Claims Mali Restaurant Attack," *Aljazeera*, March 9, 2015. As of May 19, 2015:
http://www.aljazeera.com/news/2015/03/
al-qaeda-linked-group-claims-mali-restaurant-attack-150309072613760.html

"Another Attack on a Convoy of MINUSMA Contractors," United Nations Multidimensional Integrated Stabilization Mission in Mali, April 20, 2015. As of May 19, 2015:
https://minusma.unmissions.org/en/another-attack-convoy-minusma-contractors

"AQIM Attack Against Malian Army Close to Mauritanian Border Indicates Group's Strategy to Stretch French Security Operation," *IHS Jane's Intelligence Weekly*, January 6, 2015.

Arfaoui, Jamel, "Tunisia: AQIM Claim Tunisia Attack," *Magharebia*, June 16, 2014. As of May 19, 2015:
http://allafrica.com/stories/201406170108.html

Assemblée Nationale du Mali, "Loi d'orientation et de programmation militaire," *Malijet*, February 23, 2015. As of May 20, 2015:
http://malijet.com/a_la_une_du_mali/123864-loi-d%E2%80%99oriation-et-de-programmation-militaire-un-investissemen.html

Associated Press, "Explosive Detonates in Mali's Capital, Killing 2," *New York Times*, April 3, 2015.

"Barkhane: Point du situation du 12 mars," French Ministry of Defense, March 12, 2015. As of May 20, 2015:
http://www.defense.gouv.fr/operations/actualites/
barkhane-point-de-situation-du-12-mars

"Belmokhtar's Militants 'Merge' with Mali's MUJAO," *BBC News*, August 22, 2013. As of May 19, 2015:
http://www.bbc.com/news/world-us-canada-23796920

Binnie, Jeremy, "Analysis: UN Peacekeepers Struggle Against IEDs in Mali," *IHS Jane's Defence Weekly*, January 6, 2015. As of May 20, 2015:
http://www.janes.com/article/47610/
analysis-un-peacekeepers-struggle-against-ieds-in-mali

Boilley, Pierre, *Les Touaregs Kel Adagh: Dépendances et révoltes—du Soudan français au Mali contemporain*, Paris: Karthala, 1999.

Bonkoungou, Mathieu, "Gunmen Kidnap Romanian from Burkina Faso Mine Near Mali Border," Reuters, April 4, 2015.

Bureau du vérificateur général, *Acquisition d'un aéronef et fourniture aux Forces armées maliennes de matériels d'habillement, de couchage, de campement, et d'alimentation (HCCA), ainsi que de véhicules et de pièces de rechange*, Bamako, Mali, October 2014. As of May 20, 2015:
http://www.bvg-mali.org/fichiers/2014/Rapports/MDAC_2014.pdf

Carayol, Rémi, "Mali: Les Casques bleus, cibles privilégiées des jihadistes," *Jeune Afrique*, October 23, 2014.

———, "Terrorisme au Sahel: La stratégie de Sisyphe," *Jeune Afrique*, March 24, 2015.

Central Intelligence Agency, "Mali," in *World Fact Book*, Washington, D.C., last updated June 20, 2014.

Centre de doctrine et d'emploi des forces, *Doctrine d'emploi des Forces Terrestres en zones désertique et semi-désertique (édition provisoire)*, Paris: Armée de Terre, 2013.

Chauzal, Grégory, and Thibault Van Damme, *The Roots of Mali's Conflict: Moving Beyond the 2012 Crisis*, CRU Report, Clindendael: Netherlands Institute of International Relations, 2015.

Chivvis, Chris, and Andrew Liepman, *North Africa's Menace: AQIM's Evolution and the U.S. Policy Response*, Santa Monica, Calif.: RAND Corporation, RR-415-OSD, 2013. As of October 22, 2015:
http://www.rand.org/pubs/research_reports/RR415.html

"Cinq pays du Sahel appellent l'ONU à intervenir militairement en Libye," *Le Monde*, December 19, 2014.

CIVIC—*See* Civilians in Conflict.

Civilians in Conflict, *Fending for Ourselves: The Civilian Impact of Mali's Three-Year Conflict*, Washington, D.C., 2015.

Clémenceau, François, "Le Drian: 'Daech essaie de prendre la main en Libye,'" *Le Journal du Dimanche*, updated December 30, 2014. As of May 20, 2015:
http://www.lejdd.fr/International/
Jean-Yves-Le-Drian-au-JDD-Daech-essaie-de-prendre-la-main-en-Libye-708854

"Communiqué du Conseil des ministres du mercredi 16 mai 2012," *Maliweb*, May 17, 2012. As of May 20, 2015:
http://www.maliweb.net/politique/conseil-des-ministres/
communique-du-conseil-des-ministres-du-mercredi-16-mai-2012-67093.html

Conflict Armament Research and Small Arms Survey, *Rebel Forces in Northern Mali: Documented Weapons, Ammunition and Related Material, April 2012–March 2013*, London and Geneva, April 2013.

Diarra, A., "Mali: Eucap Sahel Mali: Un soutien multiforme," *Maliactu*, 2015.

Diop, Massiré, "Mali: Suite à de violents accrochages dimanche dernier à Boulkessi; Des éléments du HCUA chassés de la localité par l'armée malienne," *L'Indépendant* (Bamako), November 4, 2015. As of May 23, 2015:
http://maliactu.net/mali-suite-a-de-violents-accrochages-dimanche-dernier-a-
boulkessi-des-elements-du-hcua-chasses-de-la-localite-par-larmee-malienne/

"L'équipe de formateurs de la batterie d'appui feu reçoit des lance-roquettes GRAD2M," European Union Training Mission in Mali, November 5, 2013. As of May 20, 2015:
http://www.eutmmali.eu/?p=1745

European Union External Action, *Common Security and Defence Policy: The EUCAP Sahel Mali Civilian Mission*, Brussels, March 2015. As of December 15, 2015:
http://eeas.europa.eu/csdp/missions-and-operations/eucap-sahel-mali/docs/factsheet_eucap_sahel_mali_en.pdf

European Union Training Mission in Mali, *Séminaire de renseignement armée de terre: Consolidation des connaissances du personnel en charge du renseignement des régions militaires et de la division renseignement de l'EMAT*, Bamako, Mali, March 11, 2015. As of May 20, 2015:
http://www.eutmmali.eu/wp-content/uploads/2015/03/20150311_BROCHURE_SEMIN_RENS1.pdf

EUTM—*See* European Union Training Mission in Mali.

Fisher-Thompson, Jim, "U.S.-African Partnership Helps Counter Terrorists in Sahel Region," IIP Digital, U.S. Department of State, March 23, 2004. As of October 22, 2015:
http://iipdigital.usembassy.gov/st/english/article/2004/03/20040323170343rlejrehsif0.1366693.html#axzz2uHqBG1jC

Florquin, Nicolas, and Stephanie Pezard, "Insurgency, Disarmament and Insecurity in Northern Mali, 1990–2004," in Nicolas Florquin and Eric Berman, eds., *Armed and Aimless: Armed Groups, Guns, and Human Security in the ECOWAS Region*, Geneva: Small Arms Survey, 2005, pp. 46–77.

Field Manual 3-07, *Stability Operations*, Washington, D.C.: Headquarters, Department of the Army, October 2008.

FM—*See* Field Manual.

"Les forces armées maliennes se dotent d'un système d'information pour la gestion de leurs effectifs," European Union Training Mission in Mali, January 23, 2014. As of April 23, 2015:
http://www.eutmmali.eu/?p=2117

"Foreigners Targeted in Mali Restaurant Attack," *Aljazeera*, March 8, 2015. As of May 19, 2015:
http://www.aljazeera.com/news/africa/2015/03/foreigners-targeted-mali-restaurant-attack-150308015450972.html

"French Forces in Mali Kill Islamist on U.S. Wanted List," Reuters, December 11, 2014. As of May 19, 2015:
http://af.reuters.com/article/topNews/idAFKBN0JP17520141211

French Ministry of Defense, *Opération Barkhane*, Paris, August 11, 2014. As of May 20, 2015:
http://www.defense.gouv.fr/operations/sahel/dossier-de-presentation-de-l-operation-barkhane/operation-barkhane

———, "Carte Operation Barkhane," Paris, updated December 3, 2015. As of December 15, 2015:
http://www.defense.gouv.fr/operations/sahel/cartes/carte-operation-barkhane

"La Garde nationale du Mali," Facebook post by Vive L'Armée Républicaine du Mali, January 8, 2013. As of July 19, 2015:
https://www.facebook.com/vivelarmeemalienne/posts/573179312695774

Goya, Michel, "La voie de l'épée: Extension du domaine de la lutte," *La Voie de l'Épée*, May 2014. As of May 20, 2015:
http://lavoiedelepee.blogspot.com/2014/05/extension-du-domaine-de-la-lutte.html

Grémont, Charles, *Tuaregs et Arabes dans les forces armées coloniales et maliennes: Une histoire en trompe-l'oeil*, Note de l'Ifri, Paris: Ifri, 2010.

"Le groupe de Mokhtar Belmokhtar revendique le double attentat au Niger," *France 24*, December 20, 2013. As of May 19, 2015:
http://www.france24.com/fr/20130524-niger-attentats-attaques-voitures-piegees-agadez-caserne-militaire-arlit-areva-mujao-mokhtar-belmokhtar

"GTIA 'Al Farouk,'" European Union Training Mission in Mali, January 28, 2015. As of May 20, 2015:
http://www.eutmmali.eu/?p=2907

Guilloteau, Christophe, and Philippe Nauche, *Rapport d'information déposé en application de l'article 145 du règlement, par la Commission de la défense nationale et des forces armées, en conclusion des travaux d'une mission d'information sur l'opération Serval au Mali*, Paris: Assemblée Nationale, Senate Report 1288, July 18, 2013. As of May 20, 2015:
http://www.assemblee-nationale.fr/14/rap-info/i1288.asp

Hall, Bruce S., *A History of Race in Muslim West Africa, 1600–1960*, Cambridge, UK: Cambridge University Press, 2011.

Hammer, Joshua, "When the Jihad Came to Mali," *New York Review of Books*, March 21, 2013. As of October 22, 2015:
http://www.nybooks.com/articles/archives/2013/mar/21/when-jihad-came-mali/?pagination=false

Harmon, Stephen A., *Terror and Insurgency in the Sahara-Sahel Region: Corruption, Contraband, Jihad and the Mali War of 2012–2013*, Burlington, Vt.: Ashgate Publishing, 2014.

Hinshaw, Drew, "Timbuktu Training Site Shows Terrorists' Reach," *Wall Street Journal*, February 1, 2013. As of May 20, 2015:
http://www.wsj.com/articles/SB10001424127887323926104578278030474477210

Hollande, François, "Allocution à la base aérienne de Niamey au Niger," Présidence de la République française, July 19, 2014. As of May 20, 2015:
http://www.elysee.fr/assets/pdf/allocution-a-la-base-aerienne-de-niamey-au-niger-2.pdf

"In memoriam," French Ministry of Defense, December 10, 2014. As of May 19, 2015:
http://www.defense.gouv.fr/operations/sahel/in-memoriam/in-memoriam

International Crisis Group, CrisisWatch Database: Mali, Brussels, undated. As of May 19, 2015:
http://www.crisisgroup.org/en/publication-type/crisiswatch/crisiswatch-database.aspx?CountryIDs=%7b00784553-1A92-4A05-8825-9235786CF9BC%7d

———, *Avoiding Escalation*, Africa Report No. 189, Brussels, July 18, 2012.

———, *Mali: La paix à marche forcée?* Rapport Afrique 226, Brussels, 2015.

International Institute for Strategic Studies, "Chapter Nine: Sub-Saharan Africa," *The Military Balance*, Vol. 115, No. 1, 2015, pp. 421–480.

IRIN—*See* Integrated Regional Information Network.

Jacinto, Leela, "Africa—Mali's Whisky-Drinking Rebel Turned Islamist Chief," *France 24*, June 29, 2012. As of July 1, 2015:
http://www.france24.com/en/20120612-northern-mali-peace-dealer-or-wrecker-nine-lives-ansar-dine-chief-iyad-ag-ghali

Joint Publication 3-24, *Counterinsurgency*, Washington, D.C.: Joint Staff, November 22, 2013.

Joint Publication 3-31, *Command and Control for Joint Land Operations*, Washington, D.C.: Joint Staff, February 24, 2014. As of May 20, 2015:
http://www.dtic.mil/doctrine/new_pubs/jp3_31.pdf

Kappès-Grangé, Anne, "L'ONU confirme les liens étroits entre Boko Haram et Aqmi," *Jeune Afrique*, January 29, 2012. As of May 20, 2015:
http://www.jeuneafrique.com/Article/ARTJAWEB20120129200338/

Kennedy Boudali, Lianne, *The Trans-Sahara Counterterrorism Partnership*, North Africa Project, West Point, N.Y.: Combating Terrorism Center, United States Military Academy, 2007.

"Kidal: Former les contingents sur le danger des mines et IED," United Nations Multidimensional Integrated Stabilization Mission in Mali, September 25, 2014. As of May 20, 2015:
https://minusma.unmissions.org/kidal-former-les-contingents-sur-le-danger-des-mines-et-ied

Lagneau, Laurent, "Sahel: Les effectifs de l'opération Barkhane vont augmenter; Deux militaires français gravement blessés au Mali," *Zone Militaire*, March 11, 2015. As of March 18, 2015:
http://www.opex360.com/2015/03/11/sahel-les-effectifs-de-loperation-barkhane-vont-augmenter-deux-militaires-francais-gravement-blesses-au-mali/

"Le lance-roquette grad équipe EUTM Mali," *Bruxelles2*, November 6, 2013. As of May 20, 2015:
http://www.bruxelles2.eu/2013/11/06/eutm-mali-equipe-de-lances-roquettes

Larcher, Laurent, "La révolte du premier bataillon malien formé par l'Union européenne," *La Croix*, June 14, 2013.

Le Bihan, Thomas, "Réussites et manques: Bilan des six premiers mois d'EUTM Mali (Lecointre)," *Bruxelles2*, July 21, 2013. As of May 20, 2015:
http://www.bruxelles2.eu/2013/07/21/
reussites-et-manques-le-bilan-des-six-premiers-mois-deutm-mali-lecointre/

Lebovich, Andrew, "The Local Face of Jihadism in Northern Mali," *CTC Sentinel*, Vol. 6, No. 6, 2013.

Lecocq, Baz, *That Desert Is Our Country: Tuareg Rebellions and Competing Nationalisms in Contemporary Mali (1946–1996)*, Amsterdam: Academisch Proefschrift, 2002.

———, *Disputed Desert: Decolonization, Competing Nationalism and Tuareg Rebellions in Northern Mali*, Leiden: Brill, 2010.

Lecocq, Baz, and Paul Schrijver, "The War on Terror in a Haze of Dust: Potholes and Pitfalls on the Saharan Front," *Journal of Contemporary African Studies*, Vol. 25, No. 1, 2007, pp. 141–166.

Lert, Frédéric, "Sahel: La guerre aride," *Science et Vie*, special issue, *Spécial Aviation*, 2015.

Lewis, David, "Top Malian Army Officer Survives Assassination Attempt in Capital: Sources," Reuters, January 26, 2015. As of May 20, 2015:
http://www.reuters.com/article/2015/01/26/
us-mali-shooting-idUSKBN0KZ2LR20150126

Lewis, David, and Emma Farge, "Dutch UN Attack Helicopters Strike Mali Rebels in North," Reuters, January 20, 2015. As of May 20, 2015:
http://www.reuters.com/article/2015/01/20/
us-mali-fighting-un-idUSKBN0KT29520150120

Maiga, Ahmadou, "Pourquoi le Gatia?" *Le Guido*, January 2015.

"Mali—Air Force," *IHS Jane's*, March 16, 2015.

"Mali—Armed Forces," Jane's Sentinel Security Assessment—North Africa, *Jane's Defence*, October 14, 2014.

"Mali Army 'Fire as Islamists Advance,'" *BBC News*, January 8, 2013. As of May 20, 2015:
http://www.bbc.com/news/world-africa-20936803

"Mali: Au moins deux membres de la famille du général ag Gamou tués," Radio France Internationale, November 21, 2013. As of May 20, 2015:
http://www.rfi.fr/afrique/
20131121-mali-moins-deux-membres-famille-general-ag-gamou-tues/

"Mali: Au moins huit soldats tués, que s'est-il passé à Nampala?" *Jeune Afrique*, January 6, 2015.

"Mali Crisis: Attack on UN Convoy Kills Two," *BBC News*, April 18, 2015. As of May 19, 2015:
http://www.bbc.com/news/world-africa-32366032

"Mali Crisis: US Admits Mistakes in Training Local Troops," *BBC News*, January 25, 2013. As of July 21, 2015:
http://www.bbc.com/news/world-africa-21195371

"Mali: Des instructeurs français dépêchés pour une formation anti-terroriste," *EnnaharOnline*, April 13, 2010. As of October 25, 2015:
http://www.ennaharonline.com/fr/international/4391.html

"Mali: En plein marché, Aqmi décapite un homme accusé de travailler pour les Français," *Jeune Afrique*, March 23, 2015.

"Mali: Indignation Dominates Reaction as Attacks in the North Escalate," Integrated Regional Information Network, August 31, 2007. As of May 20, 2015:
http://www.irinnews.org/report/74058/
mali-indignation-dominates-reaction-as-attacks-in-north-escalate

"Mali: L'armée attaquée près de la frontière mauritanienne, cinq morts," *Jeune Afrique*, January 5, 2015.

"Mali: Lawlessness, Abuses Imperil Population," Human Rights Watch, April 14, 2015. As of May 19, 2015:
http://www.hrw.org/news/2015/04/14/mali-lawlessness-abuses-imperil-population

"Mali: Mort d'un important jihadiste," Radio France Internationale, March 14, 2014. As of May 19, 2015:
http://www.rfi.fr/afrique/20140314-mali-mort-important-jihadiste-omar-ould-hamada-mujao-ansar-dine-ansar-al-charia/

"Mali: Neuf casques bleus tués," *Le Monde* with Reuters, October 3, 2014. As of May 23, 2015:
http://www.lemonde.fr/afrique/article/2014/10/03/
mali-neuf-casques-bleus-tues_4500307_3212.html

"Mali President Replaces Junta-Linked Army Chief," *Voice of America*, November 9, 2013. As of May 20, 2015:
http://www.voanews.com/content/
mali-president-repleaces-junta-linked-army-chief/1787125.html

"Mali: Qui est derrière les attaques dans le centre du pays?" Radio France Internationale, April 12, 2015. As of May 19, 2015:
http://www.rfi.fr/afrique/
20150412-deux-soldats-maliens-tues-une-attaque-le-centre-pays/

"Mali: Trois morts dans une attaque contre la Minusma à Kidal," Radio France Internationale, March 8, 2015. As of May 19, 2015:
http://www.rfi.fr/afrique/20150308-mali-morts-casque-bleu-minusma-tirs-mortiers-obus-kidal/

"Mali: Un chef djihadiste d'Al-Mourabitoun tué dans une opération française," *Le Monde*, December 11, 2014. As of May 19, 2015:
http://www.lemonde.fr/afrique/article/2014/12/11/mali-un-chef-djihadiste-d-al-mourabitoun-tue-dans-une-operation-francaise_4538809_3212.html#

"Mali: Une nouvelle attaque meurtrière visant un camp de la Minusma à Kidal," Radio France Internationale, October 8, 2014.

Mariko, Amidou, *Mémoires d'un crocodile: Du sujet français au citoyen malien*, Bamako: Éditions Donniya, 2001.

Marshall, Tyrone C., Jr., "AFRICOM Commander Addresses Concerns, Potential Solutions in Mali," U.S. Africa Command, January 24, 2013. As of December 15, 2015:
http://www.africom.mil/Newsroom/Article/10234/
general-ham-at-howard-university

McGregor, Andrew, "A Divided Military Fuels Mali's Political Crisis," *Terrorism Monitor*, Vol. 12, No. 12, June 13, 2014.

Mehta, Aaron, "Super Tucano Nets Sale to Mali," *DefenseNews*, June 15, 2015. As of November 2, 2015:
http://www.defensenews.com/story/defense/air-space/strike/2015/06/15/
super-tucano-nets-sale-to-mali-embraer/71245586/

Miles, Donna, "DefenseLINK News: New Counterterrorism Initiative to Focus on Saharan Africa," American Forces Press Service, U.S. Department of Defense, January 15, 2007. As of November 2, 2015:
http://web.archive.org/web/20070115212856/http://www.defenselink.mil/news/
May2005/20050516_1126.html

Ministerie van of Defensie (Netherlands), *NL bijdrage uitgelicht: Factsheet inlichtingen (ASIFU) MINUSMA*, The Hague, May 2014. As of May 20, 2015:
http://missiemali.nl/wp-content/uploads/2014/05/
Inlichtingen-ASIFU-MINUSMA-NL-bijdrage-uitgelicht.pdf

MINUSMA—*See* United Nations Multidimensional Integrated Stabilization Mission in Mali.

"MINUSMA Facts and Figures," United Nations Multidimensional Integrated Stabilization Mission in Mali, June 25, 2014.

"MINUSMA Facts and Figures," United Nations Multidimensional Integrated Stabilization Mission in Mali, May 19, 2015.

Mission Update Briefing," European Union Training Mission in Mali, November 17, 2014.

Morgan, Andy, "Mali's Tuareg Rebellion," *The Global Dispatches*, March 27, 2012.

Niezen, Ronald Wesley, *Diverse Styles of Islamic Reform Among the Songhay of Eastern Mali*, dissertation, Cambridge, UK: Cambridge University, 1987.

Omitoogun, Wuyi, and Eboe Hutchful, *Budgeting for the Military Sector in Africa: The Processes and Mechanisms of Control*, Solna and Oxford: Stockholm International Peace Research Institute and Oxford University Press, 2006.

Pacte national conclu entre le gouvernement de la République du Mali et les Mouvements et fronts unifiés de l'Azawad consacrant le statut particulier du Nord du Mali, Bamako: Government of the Republic of Mali and United Movement and Fronts of Azawad, April 11, 1992. As of November 2, 2015: http://news.abamako.com/documents/docs/Pacte_National_annexes.pdf

"Peacekeeping Operations," Norway Mission to the United Nations, December 17, 2014. As of May 20, 2015: http://www.norway-un.org/NorwayandUN/Norwegian-UN-Politcies/Peace_Operations/#.VVtI_WbtBGZ

Pezard, Stephanie, and Michael Shurkin, *Toward a Secure and Stable Mali: Approaches to Engaging Local Actors*, Santa Monica, Calif.: RAND Corporation, RR-296-OSD, 2013. As of November 2, 2015: http://www.rand.org/pubs/research_reports/RR296.html

———, *Achieving Peace in Northern Mali: Past Agreements, Local Conflicts, and the Prospects for a Durable Settlement*, Santa Monica, Calif.: RAND Corporation, RR-892-OSD, 2015. As of November 2, 2015: http://www.rand.org/pubs/research_reports/RR892.html

Pincus, Walter, "Mali Insurgency Followed 10 Years of U.S. Counterterrorism Programs," *Washington Post*, January 16, 2013. As of November 2, 2015: https://www.washingtonpost.com/world/national-security/mali-insurgency-followed-10-years-of-us-counterterrorism-programs/2013/01/16/a43f2d32-601e-11e2-a389-ee565c81c565_story.html

Powelson, Simon, *Enduring Engagement, Yes, Episodic Engagement, No: Lessons for SOF from Mali*, master's thesis, Monterey, Calif.: Naval Postgraduate School, 2013.

Rabasa, Angel, John Gordon IV, Peter Chalk, Audra K. Grant, K. Scott McMahon, Stephanie Pezard, Caroline Reilly, David Ucko, and S. Rebecca Zimmerman, *From Insurgency to Stability*, Vol. 2: *Insights from Selected Case Studies*, Santa Monica, Calif.: RAND Corporation, MG-1111/2-OSD, 2011. As of May 20, 2015:
http://www.rand.org/pubs/monographs/MG1111z2.html

"Réforme de l'armée: La cartographie de l'organisation territoriale de la nouvelle Armée du Mali," *Maliweb*, February 21, 2014. As of May 20, 2015:
http://www.maliweb.net/armee/reforme-de-larmee-la-cartographie-de-lorganisation-territoriale-de-la-nouvelle-armee-du-mali-197580.html

Rieussec, Sebastien, "Saharan Islamist Group Claims Responsibility for Mali Attack," *France 24*, May 14, 2015. As of May 19, 2015:
http://www.france24.com/en/20150308-saharan-islamist-group-claims-responsibility-mali-attack/

Roger, Benjamin, "Général Lecointre: 'Il faut que l'armée devienne l'un des piliers de l'État malien,'" *Jeune Afrique*, March 18, 2013. As of March 26, 2015:
http://www.jeuneafrique.com/Article/ARTJAWEB20130315174252

———, "Mali: Au moins deux soldats maliens tués dans l'attaque contre Ténenkou, près de Mopti," *Jeune Afrique*, January 16, 2015. As of May 19, 2015:
http://www.jeuneafrique.com/Article/ARTJAWEB20150116101258/

———, "Tunisie: Deux militaires tués dans une explosion au Jebel Chaambi," *Jeune Afrique*, June 6, 2013. As of May 19, 2015:
http://www.jeuneafrique.com/Article/ARTJAWEB20130606101458/

Samson, Valérie, "Un dixième soldat français tué au Mali," *Le Figaro*, October 30, 2014.

Schaefer, Agnes G., and Lynn E. Davis, *Defense Sector Assessment Rating Tool*, Santa Monica, Calif.: RAND Corporation, TR-864-OSD, 2010. As of November 2, 2015:
http://www.rand.org/pubs/technical_reports/TR864.html

Scheele, Judith, "Tribus, états et fraude: La région frontalière algéro-malienne," *Études rurales*, Vol. 2009/2, No. 184, 2009, pp. 79–94.

Shurkin, Michael, *France's War in Mali: Lessons for an Expeditionary Army*, Santa Monica, Calif.: RAND Corporation, RR-770-A, 2014. As of May 20, 2015:
http://www.rand.org/pubs/research_reports/RR770.html

Soares, B. F., "The Prayer Economy in a Malian Town (L'économie de la prière dans une ville malienne)," *Cahiers d'Études Africaines*, Vol. 36, No. 144, 1996, pp. 739–753.

———, "Islam and Public Piety in Mali," in Armando Salvatore and Dale F. Eickelman, eds., *Public Islam and the Common Good*, Leiden: Brill, 2004, pp. 205–225.

Solère Stintzy, Emmanuel de, "Terrorisme: Quand Boko Haram recrute au Cameroun," *Jeune Afrique*, September 9, 2014.

Sonner, Heather, and Kyle Dietrich, *Fending for Ourselves: The Civilian Impact of Mali's Three-Year Conflict*, Washington, D.C.: Center for Civilians in Conflict, 2015. As of May 20, 2015:
http://civiliansinconflict.org/uploads/files/
Civilian_Impact_of_Mali_3-Year_Conflict_small.pdf

Stoddard, Abby, Adele Harmer, and Kathleen Ryou, *Aid Worker Security Report 2014: Unsafe Passage; Road Attacks and Their Impact on Humanitarian Operations*, London: Humanitarian Outcomes, U.S. Agency for International Development, August 2014. As of May 20, 2015:
https://aidworkersecurity.org/sites/default/files/
Aid%20Worker%20Security%20Report%202014.pdf

Takiou, Chahana, "Evolution de la situation sécuritaire au Nord: Carnage à Aguel-Hoc," *Le 22 Septembre*, January 26, 2012.

Tardy, Thierry, "A Critique of Robust Peacekeeping in Contemporary Peace Operations," *International Peacekeeping*, Vol. 18, No. 2, April 2011, pp. 152–167.

Thiam, Adam, "Au coeur du dispositif antiterroriste d'ATT: Le Pspdn et ses hommes," *Sahara Medias FR*, July 30, 2010.

Thiénot, Dorothée, "Le blues de l'armée malienne," *Le Monde Diplomatique*, May 2013. As of May 20, 2015:
http://www.monde-diplomatique.fr/2013/05/THIENOT/49061

"Those Who Sign with Blood," GlobalSecurity.org, 2015. As of May 19, 2015:
http://www.globalsecurity.org/military/world/para/mujwa.htm

"Les touaregs du Col. Ag Gamou et l'armée française aux portes de Tessalit," video, posted to YouTube by ImazighenLibya, February 9, 2013. As of May 20, 2015:
http://www.youtube.com/watch?v=AM0xfEP7oW8

Touchard, Laurent, "CONOPS: Revue de détails; Les Forces armées maliennes de Janvier 2012 à Janvier 2013," *CONOPS*, January 15, 2013a. As of May 20, 2015:
http://conops-mil.blogspot.com/2013/01/
commentairessur-larmee-de-terre-methode.html

———, "CONOPS: Décryptage; Paris–Bamako, je t'aime, moi non plus," *CONOPS*, June 8, 2013b. As of November 2, 2015:
http://conops-mil.blogspot.fr/2013/06/
decryptage-paris-bamako-je-taime-moi.html

———, "Guerre au Mali: Retour sur le drame d'Aguelhok," *Jeune Afrique*, October 21, 2013c. As of July 19, 2015:
http://www.jeuneafrique.com/167687/politique/
guerre-au-mali-retour-sur-le-drame-d-aguelhok/

————, "Mali: Retour sur la bataille décisive de Konna," *Jeune Afrique*, January 30, 2014a. As of November 3, 2014:
http://www.jeuneafrique.com/Article/ARTJAWEB20140130165338/

————, "Armée malienne: Les affrontements de Kidal, chronique d'une déroute annoncée," *Jeune Afrique*, May 27, 2014b. As of December 15, 2015:
http://www.jeuneafrique.com/Article/ARTJAWEB20140527131237/

————, "Défense: Où en sont les Forces armées maliennes?" *Jeune Afrique*, June 11, 2014c. As of May 20, 2015:
http://www.jeuneafrique.com/Article/ARTJAWEB20140605155654/

"UN Holds Talks to Calm North Mali Town as Armed Groups Clash," *Voice of America*, January 19, 2015. As of May 18, 2015:
http://www.voanews.com/content/
reu-united-nations-talks-northern-mali-tabankort/2605173.html

United Nations, *Nouakchott Process*, United Nations Multilingual Terminology Database (UNTERM), undated. As of May 20, 2015:
http://unterm.un.org

United Nations Multidimensional Integrated Stabilization Mission in Mali, "Since the Launch of the #UN Mission in #Mali, Peacekeepers Have Been Victims of Various Types of Attacks," posted to Twitter by UN_MINUSMA, April 13, 2015a. As of May 19, 2015:
https://twitter.com/UN_MINUSMA/status/587514618144284672

————, "MINUSMA Deeply Concerned at Upsurge of Violence in the North of Mali," press release, May 19, 2015b.

United Nations Office of the High Commissioner for Human Rights, "Press Briefing Note on Yemen and Mali," April 14, 2015. As of May 20, 2015:
http://www.ohchr.org/EN/NewsEvents/Pages/
DisplayNews.aspx?NewsID=15839&LangID=E

United Nations Security Council, Resolution 2100, April 25, 2013. As of November 2, 2015:
http://www.un.org/press/en/2013/sc10987.doc.htm

————, Resolution 2164, 2014a. As of November 2, 2015:
http://www.un.org/press/en/2014/sc11453.doc.htm

————, *Report of the Secretary-General on the Situation in Mali*, New York, S/2014/943, December 23, 2014b. As of November 2, 2015:
http://www.un.org/ga/search/view_doc.asp?symbol=S/2014/943

————, *Report of the Secretary-General on the Situation in Mali*, New York, S/2015/219, March 27, 2015. As of November 2, 2015:
http://www.un.org/ga/search/view_doc.asp?symbol=S/2015/219

U.S. Government Accountability Office, *Combating Terrorism: Actions Needed to Enhance Implementation of Trans-Sahara Counterterrorism Partnership*, Washington, D.C., GAO-08-860, 2008.

———, *Combating Terrorism: U.S. Efforts in Northwest Africa Would Be Strengthened by Enhanced Program Management*, Washington, D.C., GAO-14-518, 2014.

"Véritable carnage à Kidal: Enième humiliation ou débout de la reconquête armée?" *Malijet*, May 20, 2014. As of November 2, 2015:
http://malijet.com/a_la_une_du_mali/
102194-veritable-carnage-a-kidal-enieme-humiliation-ou-debut-de-la-reco.html

"Visite du chef d'etat major de l'armée de terre au GTIA 6," *Abamako*, January 11, 2015. As of May 20, 2015:
http://news.abamako.com/v/25610.html

Warner, Lesley Anne, *The Trans Sahara Counter Terrorism Partnership: Building Partner Capacity to Counter Terrorism and Violent Extremism*, Washington, D.C.: Center for Complex Operations, 2014.

Whitehouse, Bruce, "How US Military Assistance Failed in Mali," *Bridges from Bamako*, April 21, 2014. As of July 1, 2015:
http://bridgesfrombamako.com/2014/04/21/how-us-military-assistance-failed/

"World Armies: Mali," *IHS Jane's*, October 14, 2014.

World Bank, "World Development Indicators," *World DataBank*, April 14, 2015. As of April 26, 2015:
http://databank.worldbank.org/data/
reports.aspx?source=world-development-indicators

Wulf, Eric, and Farley Mesko, *Guide to a Post-Conflict Mali*, Washington, D.C.: C4ADS, 2013.

Yossi, Diakarida, "Suite aux différentes incursions du Front de libération du Macina: Mopti, la Venise malienne, en état de psychose le week-end dernier," *L'Indépendant* (Bamako), April 21, 2015. As of May 19, 2015:
http://www.maliweb.net/echos-de-nos-regions/
suite-aux-differentes-incursions-du-front-de-liberation-du-macina-mopti-la-venise-malienne-en-etat-de-psychose-le-week-end-dernier-923992.html